TIME IS SHORT

Based on Real Events

By

Alexandra Tseplyaeva

Time Is Short

Based on Real Events

Copyright © 2025 by Alexandra Tseplyaeva

To connect, share your testimony, or request a free **digital** copy of this book:

TimeIsShort.Alexandra@gmail.com

Instagram: **@TimeIsShort.Alexandra**

Also available for FREE on Apple Books, Kobo, Barnes & Noble, and many other eBook platforms.

ISBN: 979-8-9993599-0-2

To the Almighty God,

Father, Son, and Holy Spirit—

Who transformed a skeptic into a witness,

Who turned scientific certainty into divine wonder,

And Who revealed Yourself through supernatural visions and
audible insights

when I least expected but most needed them.

Your love has compelled me to share these revelations,

Your truth has set me free,

And Your Holy Spirit has given me the courage to speak.

This testimony is but a small reflection

of Your infinite grace and mercy.

May these words serve as a beacon

for those searching in the darkness,

just as You lit the way for me.

For Your glory alone,

Through Christ Jesus our LORD and Savior.

Amen.

Table of Contents

Engagement FOCUS &TENSION in PROJECT MANAGEMENT

A SELF-HELP GUIDE TO REDUCING PROJECT FRICTION AND IMPROVING OUTCOMES

ERIK LANGE

Cover art by Shane Almgren
Typeset in Garamond
First Printing, 2025

First edition

ISBN 979-8-9869779-6-6 (ebook)
ISBN 979-8-9869779-7-3 (paperback)
ISBN 979-8-9869779-8-0 (hardcover)

Introduction

If you're searching for truth and something deeper beyond your daily routine, or if you feel like there's a missing piece that nothing seems to fill, then this book is for you. And to my already saved brothers and sisters in Christ, those who are filled with the Holy Spirit and born again, I urge you to share this message with others who may need it most, because time is short indeed.

However, if you are uncertain about your salvation, have yet to experience the presence of the Holy Spirit, lack any supernatural encounters, or doubt the existence of a living and loving God, I invite you to keep reading. I want to share with you my unexpected salvation that completely transformed my life—a salvation that revealed the profound love and acceptance of a God I once thought was distant and unapproachable.

Growing up, I had no idea what salvation meant or why it mattered. Religion wasn't part of my daily life. We didn't own a Bible in our household, and I had never read one. My parents only went to church when life got really hard—and even then, it was maybe once or twice a year, if that. So, the concept of salvation was completely foreign to me. I had never heard of it, let alone pursued it. And yet, in what I can only describe as a miraculous turn of events, I found myself saved—without even realizing it at the time. It happened unexpectedly, and I was completely unaware of what God was doing in that moment. It wasn't until I connected with other believers and began learning from them that I came to understand what had actually taken place. As I read the Bible, the full meaning of that moment became clear: I had encountered actual salvation.

This unexpected experience of salvation opened the door to an even more profound journey. God, our Holy Heavenly Father, has blessed me with life-changing encounters, revealing Himself to me through numerous supernatural visions and audible insights, all while I was fully awake and aware! These encounters have shown me glimpses of His divine presence, each one more awe-inspiring than the last.

These moments of divine revelations have been so profoundly powerful that I can no longer remain silent. Filled with the courage and inspiration of the Holy Spirit—the glorious presence of the living God—I am now compelled to share my message with anyone who is willing to listen. Before we go any further, it's important to stress that even after I was saved and filled with the Holy Spirit, I remain unbound by any religious group or denomination. My faith is not defined by religion; it is rooted in a personal relationship with Jesus Christ. I don't follow religion—I follow Jesus Christ. I am a follower of Christ, Who has revealed Himself to me in ways that go far beyond any man-made systems or traditions. It's hard to truly understand what this relationship means unless you've personally encountered God. For those who haven't experienced His presence, it may seem like just another belief or religion. But to those of us who have had a real encounter with Jesus, we know **He is not confined by religion—He is far beyond it!**

The authenticity of these encounters is not something I take lightly. These were not products of my imagination, but tangible, supernatural experiences I had while fully conscious and awake. Unlike dreams that occur during sleep, visions happen while you're awake—with your mind alert and engaged—making them vivid and impossible to dismiss. They carry weight and meaning, often delivering messages that stir your spirit and leave no room for doubt. When you encounter God like this, there's no denying His existence. The clarity and purpose of these moments reveal His presence in a way that goes beyond reason. As I sought Him through prayer and worship, He graciously responded with powerful visions and insights—divine communications that confirmed His nearness and care.

However, with the tremendous privilege of receiving such divine revelations comes a profound responsibility. Claiming these experiences as divine communications is not a matter to be taken lightly. Fabricating such encounters would not only breach personal integrity but also risk severe repercussions before God Almighty. It is a sacred trust to share these experiences, and we must be deeply aware of the gravity involved. If I were to falsely claim these encounters, the consequences would be severe, for it would break the sanctity of the divine relationship and trust. This is why I approach this testimony with the utmost seriousness and reverence.

Each of these encounters deepened my understanding of God's nature, especially His **perfect unity** as the Triune God. In each of these moments, I came face-to-face with the mystery of the Triune God—God the Father, God the Son, and God the Holy Spirit—three distinct roles, yet **One God**. Each part of God plays a unique and vital role in our salvation, yet they are **One**—perfectly united, inseparable, and deeply intertwined. As you read through this book, you'll notice that I often use these names interchangeably. Yet each role of the Triune God deserves equal praise, glory, and honor, for they are one in essence and united in their purpose of salvation for us.

Our Triune God is LOVE—our merciful, Holy Heavenly Father, the Creator of all, Who breathes His life into us. He has done so much for me, and His love—so vast, pure, and overwhelming—compels me to share this blessed treasure with you. I believe everyone deserves to know this profound truth, the formula for salvation, especially in these uncertain times.

As I share my testimony, you'll see how each part of the Triune God has shaped my faith and led me to where I am today. My hope is that as you read, you'll be inspired to **question everything** you've been taught and begin pursuing a deeper, more personal relationship with our Heavenly Father. We may not fully comprehend the mystery of the Trinity, but we can experience its truth. I know that our God is calling each of us to a communion—one that fills our hearts with a love that is eternal and a purpose that transcends this life.

When the Holy Spirit fills us, we become God's witnesses. As a witness of Jesus Christ, I know that He has called us to speak boldly about what we have experienced. In the book of Acts, chapter 1, verse 8 (1:8), He tells us, **"But you will receive power when the Holy Spirit comes on you; and you will be my witnesses in Jerusalem, ... and to the ends of the earth."** With His Holy Spirit empowering me, I am now a witness to that, and I must speak up about all I have seen, felt, and heard. In fact, it is a great privilege and joy to be a living testimony of God's glorious truth. As our LORD Jesus has commanded, **"I have made you a light for the nations, to bring salvation to the ends of the earth"** (Acts 13:47, CEV). I must share that Jesus is the only way to salvation—no one else. It is only through Jesus Christ that we can receive the gift of eternal life in Paradise. I understand that many will dismiss this truth, but my responsibility is to warn, not to convince. Those who genuinely seek the truth will surely recognize it.

Unfortunately, not everyone will immediately recognize God's truth. For many, it remains veiled. As 2 Corinthians 4:3-4 (ESV) says, **"And even if our Gospel is veiled, it is veiled to those who are perishing. In their case the god of this world (satan) has blinded the minds of the unbelievers, to keep them from seeing the light of the Gospel of the glory of Christ, Who is the Image of God."** The enemy works tirelessly to keep those who are spiritually blind from seeing the truth—the treasure of salvation through Jesus Christ alone. Even with the most powerful revelations, some will remain indifferent or dismissive. However, as 2 Corinthians 3:16 (NIV) reassures us, **"whenever anyone turns to the LORD, the veil is taken away."** This is the hope we hold onto. As a living testimony of Christ, my role is not to force belief—it is to share. For those who have open hearts, the truth will eventually become clear.

And sometimes, when the time is right, God pierces through even the thickest veil with a word so sharp, so personal, it changes everything. That's what happened to me.

It was in 2023 that I heard a message from Jesus Himself that shook me to my core: **"Time is short."** These words cut through the noise of my life with a clarity that can only be described as divine.

This message, "Time is short," goes beyond my personal experience. It's a call to all of us—including you. Jesus Himself gave us a clear mandate to boldly share the truth He has revealed to us. In Matthew 10:27 (NIV), He says, **"What**

I tell you in the dark, speak in the daylight; what is whispered in your ear, proclaim from the roofs." This call to boldly proclaim the divine truths deeply stirs my heart with urgency. The revelations I've received are not for me to keep hidden or ignore but to share, to boldly proclaim what God has shown me.

As I immersed myself in the Bible, I discovered passages that confirmed this divine urgency. In the book of Acts, chapter 2, verses 17-21 (2:17-21), it speaks of the end times when God will pour out His Holy Spirit, a time marked by visions, dreams, and signs. And here I am, having seen those very visions, received those messages, and been filled with the Holy Spirit, Who now dwells within me by the Grace of God. As you can see, these biblical prophecies are being fulfilled right before our eyes, unfolding in real time.

I know this may all sound like a fairy tale to you—I was once a skeptic too, just a couple of years ago. But I've witnessed and personally experienced the reality of what I'm sharing. Now, as a witness, I share this incredible discovery with you. Embrace this truth, and recognize the blessing that has been offered to you today!

As we begin this journey together through the pages of my testimony, I ask you to keep an open heart. My hope is that this book will inspire you, challenge you, and ultimately draw you closer to the One Who loves you more than anyone else ever could on this earth. Jesus is calling you to go ALL IN, to surrender fully to Him, and to experience the fullness of His presence and blessings in your life. God has been so gracious, and I wish everyone could experience His precious gift of the Holy Spirit for all who are willing to accept it.

With this in mind, I want to encourage you to explore additional resources that can deepen your understanding. Once you finish reading this book, I'd recommend watching a few documentaries that could help expand your perspective: **Before The Wrath** (2020), **The Coming Convergence** (2017), and **Jesus, The Soul Shepherd**. These are all available on YouTube and Prime. They're all rooted in the Bible, the true and loving instructions that were given to us by our precious Holy Creator to prepare our hearts for times like today. Ultimately, it's about embracing the truth that God sent His Son, Jesus Christ, the One and only Savior, to save the whole world from eternal punishment and separation from Him. As the Bible says in John 8:32 (NIV), **"Then you will know the truth, and the truth will set you free."** This truth—the Gospel of Jesus Christ—is the key to that freedom.

In addition, I'd love to share something that can help guide you on your spiritual journey. Be sure to check out the **ALL IN CHRIST** YouTube channel and explore the playlist **"Grace Worship Songs."** It's a place where worship music, rooted in Scripture, can draw you closer to God's presence and inspire you to deepen your connection with the divine through music. But remember, worship is just one part of the equation. Prayer—spending intentional time alone with God, pouring out your heart, and leaving space for silence to receive His revelations—is equally vital, as you will discover later in this book. Both worship and prayer are essential practices that bring us closer to God.

And yet, even with these tools at our disposal, there's still one more thing we must bring to the table: a heart that's willing to receive. As Acts 28:26–27 (NIV) says,

"You will be ever hearing but never understanding;
you will be ever seeing but never perceiving.
For this people's heart has become calloused;
they hardly hear with their ears,
and they have closed their eyes.
Otherwise they might see with their eyes,
hear with their ears,
understand with their hearts and turn,
and I would heal them."

Just as we need both worship and prayer to draw near to God, we also need open hearts and minds to receive His truth and healing.

I pray that the LORD, our God, will open your eyes to see and perceive, your ears to hear and understand, and your heart to be softened, so that you may truly recognize His truth—the truth of His salvation. As you read, I pray that you receive the **gift of repentance** and experience the **healing power** of Jesus Christ. May His love transform your heart, just as it has mine.

In the Mighty Name of our LORD Jesus Christ, I pray this.

Amen.

Chapter 1

The Mark: Choosing Between Salvation and Damnation

Before we dive into the exciting part of my salvation—and the divine visions and audible insights Jesus Christ has so graciously blessed me with—I feel led to first share a crucial warning. We're heading into a time when everyone will face a choice: accept the mark of the beast or stand firm in their faith, no matter the cost. This is not a decision to be taken lightly, for it will determine the eternal destiny of all who face it. I urge you to stay far from the mark, even if it means suffering or sacrifice.

One of the most crucial warnings in God's Word—and one that I want to emphasize with urgency—is the admonition to avoid taking the mark of the beast. It is mentioned in the final book of the Bible, **Revelation**, and its consequences are eternal. Revelation 14:9-11 (NLT) warns that anyone who accepts the mark of the beast will face God's wrath and will suffer endlessly. The passage states:

"Anyone who worships the beast and his statue, or who accepts his mark on the forehead or on the hand, must drink the wine of God's anger. It has been poured full strength into God's cup of wrath, and they will be tormented with fire and burning sulfur in the presence of the holy angels and the Lamb. The smoke of their torment will rise forever and ever, and they will have no

relief day or night, for they have worshiped the beast and his statue and have accepted the mark of his name."

This is not just a metaphor or a distant possibility; it is a real, future event that will impact every person alive. This mark will become the chief instrument through which the antichrist, also called "the beast," exerts control over the world. This individual will be a master manipulator, using his charm, intelligence, and cunning to deceive the masses. This man, who will rise to global prominence under a one-world government system, will initially appear to be a savior— someone who can bring peace to a broken world, solve financial crises, and lead nations out of turmoil.

With charisma and a silver tongue, he will win the trust of leaders and common people alike. But beneath the surface, he will be filled with hatred and contempt for God, for His Word, and for everything righteous and good. He will be "the beast," though he will never refer to himself in such a way. This individual, ultimately, will be satan incarnate—the embodiment of evil in human form, fully empowered by the forces of darkness. His reign will be marked by lies, deception, and an ever-growing thirst for power and control. He will demand global worship without mercy, using fear and force to gain allegiance. Those who choose to worship him or accept his mark will be pledging allegiance to him and to a global, tyrannical regime—rejecting Christ and sealing their eternal fate in separation from God.

The Bible makes it very clear that the mark of the beast is not just a physical symbol—it is also a spiritual and moral choice that aligns a person with evil. By taking it, individuals will be choosing to follow this man, this antichrist, over Christ Himself. It will be the **final test of allegiance**: those who remain faithful to God will refuse the mark, no matter the cost, while those who submit will be eternally separated from God. The warning is urgent—this will be a time of intense spiritual warfare, where the stakes could not be higher. The consequences of choosing the beast are severe and **irreversible**.

Once again, receiving the mark is not just a physical act—it is a spiritual alignment with the godless and lawless agenda of the antichrist. It is a personal alignment with the antichrist, against God. That is why this sin is **unforgivable**. That is why it will be met with God's wrath. You cannot be forgiven. It may seem like a solution to problems, such as survival or economic hardship, but make no mistake—it's a lie designed by satan himself to lead you into eternal damnation with him. The Bible is crystal clear that accepting the mark or worshipping this leader is a grave sin with irreversible consequences. The reality of this truth is not something I can repeat too often. So, be vigilant, stay true to the Word of God, and never underestimate the power of deception that will come in the form of this global leader.

Additionally, Revelation 13:16-18 (NIV) clearly outlines that the mark of the beast will become a forced and unavoidable reality during the end times: **"It also forced all people, great and small, rich and poor, slave and free, to receive a mark on their right hands or on their foreheads, so that they could not buy or sell unless they had the mark, which is the name of the beast or the number of its name. This calls for wisdom. Let the one who has understanding calculate the number of the beast, for it is the number of a man. That number is 666."**

This passage reveals the dire consequences of accepting the mark—not only eternal damnation but also the very real challenge of survival, as those who refuse it will be unable to buy or sell. It will be a forced decision, one that will leave no one untouched. While it may not be enforced at the beginning, similar to how the COVID-19 vaccine initially wasn't mandatory but eventually became a requirement for certain jobs, the same pattern could occur with the mark of the beast. At first, it may be presented as a voluntary choice, with a false narrative to lure people in. However, as more people comply, the pressure will increase on others to follow suit. Don't take the bait!

The choice is clear: reject the mark of the beast and remain faithful to God, knowing that your perseverance will be rewarded in the life to come. Or, tragically, face the eternal consequences of choosing the beast's mark and turning away from the one true God. In the end, the decision we make in this life echoes throughout eternity.

You may have heard about the mark of the beast before, but let me make it very clear: **Do not accept it, no matter the cost!** Even if it costs you your life, **do not accept the mark of the beast.** This is not a decision you can afford to make hastily, because it's a choice that will determine where you spend eternity—either in the presence of God or in eternal separation from Him.

While there is no consensus on the exact nature of the mark of the beast, many theories proposed by Bible scholars are grounded in the increasing influence of technology, surveillance, and global systems of control. One of the most widely discussed theories today is that the mark could take the form of an **implantable microchip** or RFID (Radio

Frequency Identification) technology. With the rise of microchips for identification, access control, and financial transactions, this idea has gained traction. Regardless of its form, the central theme of this biblical prophecy is clear: it presents a stark choice between allegiance to God and submission to the forces of evil.

Many people who've had Near Death Experiences (NDEs) around the world, from different cultures and backgrounds, all share a similar story that confirmed a prophecy found in the Bible. They describe receiving the same warnings directly from Jesus Christ. What's truly remarkable is that, despite never meeting each other, their accounts are strikingly consistent. These experiences reflect prophecies found in the Bible, especially in the book of Revelation, about the mark of the beast. These testimonies not only reveal the nature of the mark but also how it will unfold and the immense danger it presents. These individuals were shown how the mark of the beast would come to pass and how humanity must avoid it at all costs.

For those who are unfamiliar, Near-Death Experiencers (NDEs) are individuals who have had life-altering encounters with the divine, usually when they were clinically dead or very near to death. During these experiences, many report vivid phenomena such as leaving their bodies, traveling through tunnels, encountering bright lights, meeting Jesus or even loved ones who have passed on. NDEs are often characterized by deep feelings of peace, unconditional love, and a sense of profound interconnectedness. These experiences transcend cultural boundaries, leaving a lasting impact on the person's understanding of life, death, and spiritual reality.

Let me now share a summarized version of the crucial warning about the coming mark of the beast, a warning that Jesus revealed to some of these NDEs. What they saw was shocking and sobering.

Jesus Christ showed them a near future where people were voluntarily accepting what appeared to be biotechnological advancements—**small chips implanted into their hands or foreheads.** These devices were marketed as tools of convenience, security, and advanced medical innovations. Promises of a streamlined life, increased safety, and a more efficient society would make these devices seem like the natural next step in human evolution. People would be led to believe they were contributing to societal progress and improvement. The mark wouldn't initially be presented as something harmful. Instead, it would be disguised as a groundbreaking innovation. No one would openly acknowledge the **spiritual devastation** it would bring, nor would it be called the "mark" at all.

But Jesus revealed the terrifying truth behind these seemingly harmless innovations. What started as a simple convenience would gradually become the only way to function in society. It would be required to buy or sell food, access healthcare, your bank accounts, work, participate in basic daily activities, and obtain other goods and services. What struck me the most was how subtle this transition would be. It would not be an immediate, forceful action but would instead creep in quietly, like a snake slowly coiling around its prey. No dramatic announcement would declare it as the mark of the beast. Instead, it would be wrapped in promises of progress and prosperity, disguised as the solution to the world's problems.

What is even more shocking is that many would eagerly accept this system, including believers who had studied the Bible their entire lives. They had expected something obvious, something overtly evil, but the deception came disguised as progress and enhancement. The enemy would use humanity's desire for progress and convenience to lure them in. The mark would promise peace, security, and even salvation in the form of solving economic, healthcare, and societal problems. It would seem like a friend, not an enemy.

Notice how the enemy, satan, is incredibly cunning. He knows that sudden and obvious changes would alarm people, so he works gradually, subtly, wrapping deception in beautiful packaging. The enemy comes as an "angel of light," offering solutions to problems, promising to make life much better. But behind those solutions lies a deep, spiritual trap. The enemy uses good intentions to lead people astray.

The systems of this world would be structured in a way that primarily targets the younger generation. The enemy mostly targets the young because he knows they will accept without a question what their elders might scrutinize. A whole generation is being prepared to accept what is coming. They would be taught from a young age that these implants are natural parts of their lives, as fundamental as any other part of their bodies. They would be encouraged to trust the devices over their own instincts, their parents' wisdom, and ultimately, even God's Wisdom.

This is heartbreaking, but it's happening. People will be blind to the eternal consequences, focusing only on the surface benefits of convenience. They will fail to see how the mark affects them spiritually, how it erodes their ability to perceive spiritual truth. They will only see the temporary advantages of the system but will ignore its devastating spiritual cost.

The mark will likely start as a voluntary program, but gradually, it will become a requirement for participation in daily life. Those who refuse will first face inconvenience, then discrimination, and eventually, persecution. Yet, Jesus showed the NDEs something beautiful: the faithful communities of believers who chose to reject the mark. These believers stood firm with a strength that could only come from above. They created alternative systems of support and commerce— simpler yet freer—holding firm to their faith despite the growing pressure to conform. They demonstrated an unwavering commitment to God's truth, relying on each other and their faith in Christ to navigate a world increasingly hostile to their beliefs.

This biotechnology will be implemented in various ways across the world, each tailored to local cultures, but always with the same goal: to create dependency and control. In some places, it will be presented through healthcare, in others through financial incentives, or even through social pressure and the fear of being left behind. In every case, however, the message will be the same: this is progress, this is necessary, this is good. Watch out for any technology that promises to make us **"better" than how God created us.** The enemy will offer enhancements to the human mind and body, but they will come at the eternal cost of our souls.

The mark will offer a solution to the global economic crisis, promising security and universal access to resources. It will be marketed as a way to protect children, the elderly, and the vulnerable in an increasingly dangerous world. It will promise to end various crimes, human trafficking, and illegal immigration. In healthcare, it will promise perfect health monitoring and automatic treatment. Many trusted leaders—religious, political, and cultural—will endorse it, arguing that it can't possibly be the mark of the beast because it doesn't demand a denial of Christ, nor does it involve worship or allegiance to anyone or anything. They will argue that it is merely technology—at least, that's what they believe.

But Jesus made it very clear: the power of the mark doesn't lie in its technology, but in what accepting it represents. It would be the ultimate choice between trusting human systems or trusting and relying on our Almighty Creator alone.

Those who question the system will be marginalized. They will be dismissed as conspiracy theorists, anti-progress, or simply afraid of change. Even in churches, people who raise concerns will be called paranoid or lacking faith. The coming global crisis will make digital currency seem necessary, while escalating natural disasters and global wars will make tracking and identification seem like practical solutions. A movement toward global unity will make resistance to the system appear selfish and dangerous. But the truth remains: we must be discerning.

Jesus revealed the eternal consequences of accepting the mark. This is not just about earthly convenience and safety; this is about **eternal souls**. The mark will **fundamentally change** those who accept it, severing their connection to God in a way that cannot be undone. Gradually, their ability to perceive spiritual truth will diminish, and their hearts will harden, not suddenly, but progressively. Ultimately, they will become like robots—numb, unable to perceive God or respond to His calling. By trading their **free will**, they will compromise their ability to choose Jesus and accept God's salvation freely. Instead, they will opt for temporary comforts that ultimately lead to eternal punishment, rejecting the gift of eternal life in perfect love and peace in heaven. No convenience on this earth is worth our soul.

But there is a blessed assurance. Jesus promises to protect and provide for those who remain faithful, just as He did for the Israelites in the wilderness. Jesus' people will not be abandoned. He will give supernatural protection, peace, and provision. Holy angels will surround His faithful, protecting them from any harm. There will be a divine renewal of strength, as Christ promised in the book of Isaiah 40:31 (NKJV): **"But those who wait on the LORD shall renew their strength; they shall mount up with wings like eagles, they shall run and not be weary, they shall walk and not faint."**

People who refused the mark will have peace that would make no sense in their circumstances. Most importantly, their relationship with Jesus will grow deeper and stronger during hardships. He also revealed how the world system will progressively grow more antagonistic toward God's ways and our God-given free will. Yet, amid this opposition, many will still recognize the truth and turn to Christ. Every small act of faith, no matter how seemingly insignificant, will ripple out in ways beyond our comprehension, touching the lives and hearts of many. For those who endure to the end, the reward in heaven will be beyond the grasp of our limited human understanding—an eternal glory in Paradise that defies earthly description.

This is not just about avoiding a future tragedy for yourself; it's also about **warning others** and spreading this truth to as many people as you possibly can. Jesus Himself commands us to go into the world and make disciples, teaching them the truth about salvation and the consequences of rejecting Him. We have a responsibility to care about what happens to others' souls after they die, because eternity is a long time.

Regardless of who you are—whether you have been a believer for your entire life or are just beginning to explore the truth—it is essential that you understand this. It is urgent! The time is short, and the stakes are higher than most people realize. The enemy, satan, is relentless in his efforts to deceive and distract you from the truth, but you must stand firm in your faith, resist temptation and doubt, and remain unwavering.

This isn't to frighten you, but to draw you closer to our God Almighty. You don't have to be afraid because you now know what is going to happen. Seek God with all your heart. In your prayer times, **ask Him to reveal these truths to you, and be persistent in your pursuit.** I promise you that God will honor your search. The urgency of this message cannot be overstated—your eternity depends on it. And I care too much about where your soul will spend eternity not to share it with you.

Moreover, it's about gaining knowledge and preparing our hearts. God's people are perishing for the lack of knowledge. This is not about convincing anyone. The choice is still yours, but our duty is to share this warning with as many people as possible because many are unaware of the big deception that is coming. The most important thing to understand is that the mark of the beast will not come as an obviously evil system that's easy to reject; it will be a solution to real problems, embraced by the masses, and endorsed by leaders we trust. The antichrist, the man behind this system, will not appear as a figure of darkness or malevolence. In fact, he will be charming, persuasive, and appear to have all the answers. His rise will seem like a beacon of hope and peace to a broken world, making the deception all the more dangerous. The world will not see him as the evil force he truly is—his cunning and manipulative nature will hide behind a facade of charisma and leadership. The deception will be subtle, which is why asking God for spiritual discernment is so crucial today.

Jesus will provide for those who remain faithful. He will give wisdom to those who seek it, strength to those who ask, and provision to those who trust Him. The challenges ahead will be great, but they will also be filled with unprecedented moves of God's Spirit. This is a call to prepare our hearts, deepen our faith, strengthen our communities, and, most importantly, develop such a close relationship with Jesus that we can hear His voice clearly when critical decisions must be made. For those who remain faithful until the end, victory is assured.

Eternal salvation or eternal damnation? This is the ultimate choice that defines our destiny. When the time comes, may we all choose wisely! In the Almighty Name of Jesus Christ, we ask this. Amen!

Now that you've been warned, let's first address a couple of important questions before I share the story of my accidental salvation.

Chapter 2

Why Do We Need to Be Saved?

In this chapter, I want to address three foundational questions that often arise:

1. Why do we need to be saved in the first place?
2. Why must we believe only in Jesus Christ as our Savior—why is He the only way to salvation?
3. And why is being filled with the Holy Spirit (born again) essential to our salvation?

To understand the answers, we must begin by examining the condition of humanity without Christ and the profound transformation that takes place through salvation.

In the beginning, before the deception by the serpent, Adam and Eve existed in a state of perfect harmony, peace, and innocence. They lived in unbroken fellowship with God, fully aware of His love and goodness. They were without sin and had no knowledge of evil, experiencing complete unity with each other and with their Holy Creator. Their lives were marked by joy, tranquility, and fulfillment, free from fear, shame, or suffering. This state of perfection reflected God's original design for humanity, where they were meant to live in an intimate relationship with Him, stewarding His creation in harmony.

However, this perfect state was disrupted when Adam and Eve chose disobedience over God's command. In Genesis 3, their fall introduced sin into the world, breaking their fellowship with God and setting humanity on a path of spiritual separation from Him. From that moment, sin has been passed down through every generation. As Romans 3:23 (NIV) states, **"for all have sinned and fall short of the glory of God."** This broken relationship with our Creator is the very root of our need for salvation.

The Apostle Paul paints a sobering picture of this fallen condition in Romans 3:10–18 (NIV):

> **"There is no one righteous, not even one;**
> **there is no one who understands;**
> **there is no one who seeks God.**
> **All have turned away,**
> **they have together become worthless;**
> **there is no one who does good,**
> **not even one.**
> **Their throats are open graves;**
> **their tongues practice deceit.**
> **The poison of vipers is on their lips.**
> **Their mouths are full of cursing and bitterness.**
> **Their feet are swift to shed blood;**
> **ruin and misery mark their ways,**
> **and the way of peace they do not know.**
> **There is no fear of God before their eyes."**

This passage might sound intense—and it is—but it honestly reflects the human condition **without** God. It's not just theological language; it's a description of the inner conflict and brokenness we often see in ourselves and in the world. These verses are not meant to condemn us, but to wake us up to our deep need for healing and restoration. God shows us our condition not to shame us, but **to lead us to**

the cure: His love, mercy, and forgiveness through Jesus Christ.

Without salvation, we are spiritually disconnected from God—the very source of true life. **Sin separates us from this source of life**, keeping us from the relationship we were created to have with Him. As Ephesians 2:1–3 (NIV) explains, **"You were dead in your transgressions and sins, in which you used to live when you followed the ways of this world... gratifying the cravings of our flesh."**

This "spiritual death" doesn't mean physical death, but a deep separation from God that affects our hearts, our decisions, and ultimately, our eternity. Without God's rescue through Jesus, we remain on a path that leads to lasting separation from Him—what the Bible describes as eternal punishment. But here's the good news—the best news of all: God made a way back for us through repentance and faith in Jesus Christ.

This spiritual separation is not just a personal struggle— it's reflected all around us. The brokenness, unrest, and heartache we witness in the world aren't random or without meaning—they reflect deeper, unseen spiritual influences and warfare at work. We are living in the midst of a spiritual battle—a war for souls, truth, and identity. As humanity drifts further from its Creator, the consequences of this separation begin to surface everywhere: in families, in communities, and in our own hearts. What we see around us—division, confusion, violence, self-centeredness—isn't just a social or political problem. It's the fallout of a deeper, invisible spiritual war being waged in these last days.

Scripture doesn't leave us guessing about this. It offers a clear description of what this looks like. In 2 Timothy 3:1–5 (NKJV), it's written: **"But know this, that in the last days perilous times will come: For men will be lovers of themselves, lovers of money, boasters, proud, blasphemers, disobedient to parents, unthankful, unholy, unloving, unforgiving, slanderers, without self-control, brutal, despisers of good, traitors, headstrong, haughty, lovers of pleasure rather than lovers of God…"**

It's hard to read—but doesn't it sound familiar? These verses read like a reflection of our world today. The chaos we see is not meaningless—it is evidence of a spiritual reality many don't even realize they're caught in. And the reason? It's been cleverly normalized by the enemy. Satan doesn't always show up with horns and a pitchfork—he shows up through culture, trends, and lies wrapped in shiny packaging. What once would've shocked us now barely raises an eyebrow. We scroll past brutality, laugh at mockery of God, and celebrate self-centeredness as empowerment. It's so subtle, so constant, that many of us don't even notice it anymore. The enemy's goal isn't just rebellion—it's blindness. And sadly, for many, it's working.

God doesn't reveal this to discourage us—He reveals it to awaken us. He shows us the battle so He can invite us into victory. Into wholeness. Into life. Into Himself.

These warnings aren't about judgment for judgment's sake. They are acts of love—God's way of saying, **"This is not the life I created you for. Come back to Me, My beloved children. Come back to the One Who truly loves you!"** They remind us how desperately we need a Savior— not just to save us from judgment, but to restore us into the life-giving relationship we were always meant to have with God. And that is why **salvation is not optional; it's essential.**

So, why must we believe **only** in Jesus Christ as our Savior—why is He **the only way** to salvation?

Because Jesus Christ is not merely a great teacher or prophet, but **God in the flesh**. 1 John 5:20 affirms that Jesus is **"the true God and eternal life."** He came to earth and took on human form in order to rescue us from the consequences of our sin. He took our sin upon Himself—the very weight that should have crushed us. We were the ones who deserved that punishment, that death—but in an act of sacrificial love, Jesus stepped in and suffered it for us. Jesus is **the only One** Who lived a **holy, sinless life in the flesh** here on earth and then willingly **died in your place**. No one else in history has ever done this! The punishment that was meant for you—He took upon Himself. He did it so that you could be set free and walk in victory. As Romans 6:23 declares, **"For the wages of sin is death, but the gift of God is eternal life in Christ Jesus our LORD."** Jesus paid the price we could never pay on our own.

But it didn't just end at the cross. Three days after His death, Jesus rose from the grave. He conquered sin, death, and hell. Hell could not hold Him—because He was without sin. His name was not written in the record of the guilty. Satan could not find any fault in Him—no accusation to bring, no sin to attach, no legal right to claim Jesus as his own. Jesus Christ overcame death and hell—He holds the keys to both now. As Revelation 1:18 (NKJV) confirms: **"I AM He Who lives, and was dead, and behold, I AM alive forevermore. Amen. And I have the keys of Hades and of**

Death." No other leader in all of history has defeated death—**only Jesus**. And He did it for you.

When you put your faith in Him and ask God for forgiveness of your sins (repentance), everything Christ accomplished—His perfect life, His sacrificial death, and His victorious resurrection—is credited to you! Romans 4:24 (NIV) says: **"But also for us, to whom God will credit righteousness—for us who believe in Him Who raised Jesus our LORD from the dead."**

Isn't it incredible how simple—and yet how powerful—God's forgiveness really is? When we believe in Jesus and genuinely ask for forgiveness of our sins, God wipes our slate completely clean. Just like that! The moment we place our faith in Christ and repent, He no longer holds anything against us. Instead of judgment, we receive mercy. Instead of guilt, we are given grace. He declares us righteous (right with God)—not because of anything we've done to earn it, but entirely because of what Jesus did for us. It's almost hard to believe—yet it's beautifully, powerfully true!

Once we are forgiven, we are made right with God—and that restored relationship gives us the promise of eternal life with Him in heaven. God no longer sees our guilt; **He sees Jesus in us and His righteousness covering us.** This is what it means to be made right with God: not through our own efforts, but by **recognizing that we are all sinners** and placing our **faith** in Jesus Christ alone.

Jesus Himself makes this exclusive claim in John 14:6–7 (NKJV): **"I AM the way, the truth, and the life. No one comes to the Father except through Me. If you had known Me, you would have known My Father also; and**

from now on you know Him and have seen Him." This is why we must believe in Jesus—not as one of many paths, but as **the only path** to God. Why? Because He alone is the Savior Who lived a holy life, died willingly for our sins, rose victoriously from the dead, and now offers eternal life to all who place their faith in Him. There is no substitute for Jesus—He is the only One Who can reconcile us to the Father for eternity.

This path is not exclusive because believers want it to be—it's exclusive because **only Jesus** dealt with the problem of sin, conquered death, and rose again. He is the only One Who made a way for all people to be saved and to experience the abundant life that only He, as the eternal God, can give.

John 3:16 captures the very heart of the Gospel: **"For God so loved the world that He gave His One and only Son, that whoever believes in Him shall not perish but have eternal life."** Let that sink in—God loves **you** so much that He gave up His one and only Son to die in **your** place. It wasn't just for the world in general—it was personal. He saw your soul as worth saving. Jesus took on the punishment you and I deserved, so that we could live forever with Him. That's how much God loves you. Not because you earned it, but simply because you are His—and He would rather die than live without you.

Because of our sin, we are completely incapable of bridging the gap between ourselves and God. But Jesus— through His sinless life, atoning death, and triumphant resurrection—became that bridge. Romans 5:8 further confirms, **"But God demonstrates His own love for us in this: While we were still sinners, Christ died for us."** His willing sacrifice on the cross, as God in the flesh, paid the penalty we could never pay. Without that sacrifice, we would still be under the penalty of sin, which is eternal death (Romans 6:23). But through Jesus, we are offered the gift of eternal life and reconciliation with God.

By coming in the flesh, Jesus not only revealed God's nature to us—He made the ultimate act of love and grace possible. He is the One and only mediator between God and humanity. Through His death and resurrection, Jesus opened the only path that leads us back to the Father. **No one else has ever done that.**

You might wonder, "Why can't I just believe in God without Jesus?" That's a fair and honest question. But believing in God alone isn't enough if we reject the very way He **chose to reveal Himself to us**. God has made Himself fully known through Jesus Christ—and He has made Jesus the only way to be reconciled to Him. This truth is clearly laid out in Colossians 1:19–23 (NLT):

"For God in all His fullness was *pleased to live in* Christ, and through Him God reconciled everything to Himself. He made peace with everything in heaven and on earth by means of Christ's blood on the cross. This includes you who were once far away from God. You were His enemies, separated from Him by your evil thoughts and actions. Yet now He has reconciled you to Himself through the death of Christ in His physical body. As a result, He has brought you into His own presence, and you are holy and blameless as you stand before Him *without a single fault*. But you *must* continue to believe this truth and stand firmly in it. Don't drift away from the assurance you received when you heard the Good News."

We **aren't** made right with God through various religions.

We **aren't** saved through New Age beliefs or spiritual philosophies.

We **don't** earn salvation through personal effort or good behavior.

We are reconciled to God through a restored relationship—and that relationship is only made possible through Jesus Christ.

Christ is **God in the flesh—God with us.** We don't come to the Father by climbing a spiritual ladder or proving ourselves worthy. We come through Jesus, the One Who paid the price in full and bridged the gap between heaven and earth, once and for all.

So no, it's not enough to simply believe in a vague, distant "higher power." Real salvation doesn't come from believing in a distant God—it comes from **knowing** the God Who came to save us. And His name is Jesus Christ.

But how do we actually walk in that relationship with God? How do we live out the new life we've been given through Jesus?

That's where the Holy Spirit comes into play.

What is the role of the Holy Spirit in salvation?

Being filled with the Holy Spirit is not just a side benefit of salvation—it's essential to it. Romans 8:9-11 (NIV) makes this clear: **"You, however, are not in the realm of the flesh but are in the realm of the Spirit, if indeed the Spirit of God lives in you. And if anyone *does not* have the Spirit of Christ, *they do not belong to Christ*. But if Christ is in**

29

you, then even though your body is subject to death because of sin, the Spirit gives life because of righteousness. And if the Spirit of Him Who raised Jesus from the dead is living in you, He Who raised Christ from the dead will also give life to your mortal bodies because of His Spirit Who lives in you."

This means that the Holy Spirit is not optional—He is the very evidence that we belong to Christ. When we accept Jesus as our LORD and Savior and turn from our old ways, the Holy Spirit comes to live within us. He doesn't just dwell with us; He fills us with new life, the same resurrection power that raised Christ from the dead. He **enables** us to walk in righteousness, leads us into truth, and strengthens our connection with the Father. The Holy Spirit is not just our helper or guide—He is the very presence of God living within us.

Our bodies become temples where the Holy Spirit dwells, guiding us into all truth and helping us fulfill the spiritual purpose God has for each of us. Without the Spirit of Christ living in us, we remain spiritually disconnected—unable to fully know God or live the life He intended.

History itself has proven that, apart from the Holy Spirit, humanity is lost. We cannot find salvation or true direction on our own. The brokenness in the world around us is living proof of what happens when people try to live without God's Spirit.

Never before has God's supernatural power been more visible than it is today, as He continues working to restore us to our original design—before Adam and Eve's fall brought sin and its curse into the world. The stakes could not be higher: without the Holy Spirit, we face eternal separation from God.

We are living in remarkable times—witnessing God's power unfold in ways our ancestors only dreamed of. His deepest desire is reconciliation with humanity. When He gives us the Holy Spirit, He begins a supernatural work within us: purifying us from sin, healing our brokenness, and transforming us from the inside out. This process continues throughout our lives, until we are fully restored to a perfect union with Him—just as Adam and Eve once were—united, unhindered, and completely at peace in His presence.

Jesus Himself emphasized the necessity of the Holy Spirit for entering God's Kingdom. In John 3:5–6, He said: **"Very truly I tell you, no one can enter the Kingdom of God unless they are born of water and the Spirit. Flesh gives birth to flesh, but the Spirit gives birth to Spirit."** Being born of the Spirit is a spiritual rebirth—it's not symbolic. It marks the beginning of a new life, empowered and led by God.

It's essential to understand: being born of the Spirit is not just a step in the salvation journey—it is the foundation of it. Without the Holy Spirit, we cannot enter the Kingdom of Heaven. Embracing His presence is key to genuine faith, enabling us to reflect God's love, power, and truth in every part of our lives.

The Holy Spirit also serves as the seal of our salvation. Ephesians 1:13–14 says, **"And you also were included in Christ when you heard the message of truth, the Gospel of your salvation. When you believed, you were marked in Him with a seal, the promised Holy Spirit, Who is a**

deposit guaranteeing our inheritance until the redemption of those who are God's possession." The Holy Spirit seals us as God's own and guarantees our eternal inheritance. That seal is God's declaration that we belong to Him. Redemption means we've been purchased—rescued from darkness (hell) and brought into God's Kingdom. Through the Holy Spirit, we are daily reminded that our salvation is secure and our future is held in God's hands.

And it's not only about the afterlife—the Holy Spirit fills us now so we can live a victorious life in this broken world. He empowers us to follow God's will, to bear spiritual fruit, and to live as witnesses of the truth. John 15:5 says, **"I AM the vine; you are the branches. If you remain in Me and I in you, you will bear much fruit; apart from Me you can do nothing."** Galatians 5:22–23 shows what this fruit looks like: **"love, joy, peace, forbearance, kindness, goodness, faithfulness, gentleness and self-control. Against such things there is no law."**

Without the Holy Spirit, we miss out on the fullness of God's presence and power in our lives.

So, to summarize: We need salvation because sin separates us from God.
Jesus provides salvation through His death and resurrection. And the Holy Spirit enables us to live it out, sealing our identity and empowering us for the journey.

Acts 2:38 calls us to respond: **"Repent and be baptized, every one of you, in the name of Jesus Christ for the forgiveness of your sins. And you will receive the gift of the Holy Spirit."** When we receive Jesus and are filled with

His Spirit, we are saved, transformed, and made new—able to walk in the power and freedom He promises.

We are called to be vessels of hope, peace, and reconciliation—shining His marvelous light into a world that desperately needs it. The Holy Spirit testifies about Jesus and continually reminds us of who we are: redeemed, adopted children of God.

So let us open our hearts to His guidance, trusting that He will lead us faithfully—sealing us with His presence until the day we stand face to face with our LORD Jesus Christ in glory. On that day, we will be fully transformed, receiving glorified, imperishable bodies (Philippians 3:20–21, 1 Corinthians 15:52–53), and forever dwell with Him in perfect joy, peace, and unending life.

Sounds too good to be true? That's the beauty of the Gospel—it *is* far more than we deserve, yet it's entirely true because God is that good. He made a way through Jesus, and He sealed that promise with His Holy Spirit. This isn't just theology—it's reality. A reality I didn't find by striving or achieving, but by crying out for help at the end of myself. I stumbled into the truth that countless people spend their whole lives searching for—and it was more real, more powerful, and more life-changing than anything this world could ever offer.

In the next chapter, I'll walk you through how this truth became undeniable in my life. It wasn't planned, polished, or perfect—but it was real. And it changed everything.

Chapter 3

Crying Out for Help: The Road to My Salvation

As we prepare to explore this chapter, I encourage you to take a moment to listen to **"Same God" by Elevation Worship**. This powerful song beautifully captures the essence of reaching out to God in times of desperation and need. It reminds us that the same God Who was present in biblical times is with us today, ready to hear our cries and support us through our struggles. As you listen, allow the lyrics to draw you closer to God, creating a sacred space where you can pour out your heart and express your deepest longings in prayer. After this heartfelt outpouring, take a moment to sit in silence, giving the LORD our God space to respond. In those quiet moments, you may discover the gentle messages of His presence or visions, offering comfort, guidance, and reassurance that you are not alone in your journey.

In my own life, it was in this very pursuit of connection with God that I found myself on the path to salvation. In the face of difficult and heartbreaking circumstances, I was left with no choice but to seek God earnestly, with all my heart and everything I had left in me. At times, it felt like the entire world was against me—like the weight of oppression, isolation, and loneliness was too much to bear. With each passing day, I began to carry the weight of unforgiveness, anger, fear, and sorrow in my heart. Eventually, I reached a breaking point where navigating life alone felt impossible. Every decision I made seemed to lead to disaster, leaving me feeling utterly hopeless. I even found myself silently contemplating suicide—thoughts I later realized were **not** my own. **They were lies from the devil, attempting to push me to end my life** *before* **I found salvation**, giving him more legal grounds to claim my soul (which I'll explain more fully later in this book). It was during this dark and desperate time that I began crying out to God, **praying persistently and humbly for over a year**, with no expectations—only a deep yearning for any sign of His existence. Every chance I got, I would close my eyes and fervently pray the Our Father—the LORD's Prayer—over and over again:

"Our Father in heaven, Holy is Your name. Your Kingdom come, Your will be done—on earth as it is in heaven. Give us today our daily bread. And forgive us our sins, as we forgive those who sin against us. And do not let us fall into temptation, but deliver us from evil. For Yours is the Kingdom, and the Power, and the Glory, now and forever more.

Please save me and keep me. Please fill me with Your Holy Spirit.

In the name of the Father, the Son, and the Holy Spirit."

Amen.

After each prayer, I would repeat this last phrase at least three times: **"Please save me and keep me. Please fill me with Your Holy Spirit."** My grandmother taught me this practice when I was a child, but at the time, I didn't understand the full significance of those words. It wasn't until I experienced salvation that I realized I had been pleading for it all along, without even knowing it. As I mentioned before, I

35

had no knowledge of God's plan of salvation—I hadn't even heard of it. And in those desperate times, the only prayer I knew and remembered was this one. After repeating this prayer, sometimes multiple times a day, I would sit in complete silence with my eyes closed, longing to receive any sign of God's existence.

I want to start by clearing something up that might make some of you skeptical—something I was once doubtful of, too, before finding Christ. First off, I don't use drugs or alcohol, and I wasn't asleep or dreaming during these experiences. I was wide awake and conscious when all my divine encounters occurred. Moreover, I received numerous confirmations of these visions through audible messages from Jesus, other believers, and the Word of God. As you will discover later in this book, Jesus also spoke through my 2-year-old daughter at the time to reassure me that I had not lost my mind. Now, with that out of the way, let me recount the incredible moment when, after months of fervent prayer and meditation on the LORD's prayer, God responded in a way that both shocked and incredibly exhilarated me.

In my broken state, I had been seeking answers with an intensity I had never felt before, yearning to know if God was truly real. **For over a year**, I made every effort to pray whenever I could, seeking solitude and freedom from interruptions at every opportunity. I dedicated myself to setting aside every hindrance—fear, worry, doubt, and cynicism—all of it was laid aside. Hope was all I had left. In that space of hope, I focused solely on the Triune God: the Father, the Son, and the Holy Spirit. I prayed earnestly and without interruption for at least an hour or two, meditating deeply and repeatedly reciting the LORD's Prayer, letting its words fill my mind and soul.

It was in this state of pleading, as I prayed with my eyes closed, that something extraordinary happened. To my absolute shock, I saw three vivid images appearing before me: a retro twin-bell alarm clock, glorious golden circles around each other, and a stunning emerald green butterfly. It was as if God had opened a window into another dimension, revealing symbols that were both mysterious and deeply meaningful. I remember the thrill of excitement and awe that surged through me. Here was God, revealing Himself in a way I had never imagined possible!

This wasn't a fleeting moment; it felt as if time itself had paused. I was engulfed in wonder as each image seemed to carry a unique resonance. I instantly sensed their significance, knowing they were rich with meaning. The imagery of the glorious golden circles, the twin-bell alarm clock, and the green butterfly speaks volumes about the transformation God has initiated in my life, urging me to embrace change and put it into action. The endless loops of the circles reminded me of the cycles of metamorphosis, a powerful sign that it was **God's appointed time** for a profound shift. Like a caterpillar undergoing its stages before becoming a butterfly, this vision revealed that my journey had reached a pivotal moment—a call to awaken, transform, and fully step into the growth and purpose God had prepared for me.

The emerald green butterfly, symbolizing resurrection and renewal, seemed to embody God's promise of rebirth. It felt as though He was revealing that, through His guidance, I was being called to shed an old identity and embrace a vibrant, renewed life—much like a butterfly emerging from its cocoon with vibrant wings. Seeing these images felt like God was encouraging me to seek further and trust that He reveals Himself in ways that are beyond our understanding.

Shortly after receiving that first vision, God didn't stop there—He gave me a powerful confirmation. I was in a store, picking out a gift for my friend's daughter, whose family had just moved into a new house in Flagstaff, about a two-hour drive from where I live. As I stood there, debating which birthday card to choose, I glanced toward the register and noticed there was only one cashier and one customer checking out. Suddenly, out of nowhere, I received what I can best describe as a "download"— a complete conversation that played out in my mind, one that was soon to take place between the cashier and me. I heard our entire future conversation before it even happened! In my mind, I heard her say, "Oh, you're going to Flagstaff." Surprised, I replied, "How did you know I was going to Flagstaff?" She simply answered, "I don't know. Lucky guess?"

When I finished choosing the card and the gift, which had nothing to do with the Flagstaff theme, I went to check them out. To my greatest astonishment, the conversation played out exactly as I heard it in my head! I was speechless. This was a powerful validation that I was meant to drive to Flagstaff that same day— or was it just a lucky guess?

When I arrived in Flagstaff, my friend took me on a tour of their new home and a large garage where the previous owners had **worked on wood.** What I saw in that garage left me in awe. There, next to the door, was an old retro twin-bell alarm clock—the exact same one from my vision! And on the inside of the door was a sign that read: **"Behold, I AM coming soon! - Jesus"** with three crosses on it. Instantly, a profound sense of peace and joy overtook me. I couldn't believe my eyes. Jesus had left me a message through the previous homeowners. Jesus was a **carpenter,** which made the place where these messages were left even more meaningful. The significance of this moment was overwhelming! It was an undeniable confirmation of my vision and a reminder of His constant loving presence.

These experiences didn't just stop there; they were the beginning of numerous unbelievable blessings! They brought me to an undeniable revelation of the existence of our Triune God. Since that day, and still to this day, Jesus has been continually unveiling Himself to me through supernatural visions and audible messages—each one received while I was fully awake and alert. These visions became the doorway to countless prophetic insights, each revelation confirming the last. They completely shattered my preconceived notions, as I had previously believed such experiences only occurred in movies! But now, I know beyond any doubt that God is real—and He reveals Himself to those who truly seek Him, often in ways we could never predict or fully comprehend.

Chapter 4

Filled with God's Spirit. SEALED. ADOPTED. SAVED

In just about two months since my visions began, I am now so happy to share with you the next most extraordinary experience of my life—getting filled with the Holy Spirit, which left me both awestruck and invigorated! It was a moment that truly felt like it couldn't get any better, and little did I know, it was only the beginning. But before I share that incredible experience, I want to remind you, my dear reader, that this is not a fictional story—it's a real-life account of my personal experience with salvation. At the time, the concept of salvation was completely foreign to me; I had never heard of it, nor did I understand what it truly meant. Remarkably, I found myself saved without even realizing it—it was purely accidental! With no prior knowledge or understanding of salvation, I was about to learn firsthand what it truly meant.

It all started when I was deeply immersed in a project, overwhelmed by a looming deadline. The pressure was immense, and despite my best efforts, panic began to set in. In that moment of desperation, I turned to God in prayer, asking for His divine strength to help me. Just when I thought I couldn't bear it any longer, something astonishing began to happen.

Out of nowhere, my chest started to expand in a way that defied all physical possibilities. My chest was rising and swelling to the point where it reached my chin! I was hyperventilating with a sense of panic, struggling to understand the magnificent sensation that was overtaking my body. It was surreal—my chest was expanding beyond its natural limits, yet I could breathe more freely than ever before—ten times better, in fact!

Then, in a dramatic shift, an intense burning sensation erupted on my forehead. It was as if a fiery touch had brushed against me, igniting my entire being. This burning sensation was so unexpected that it made me lift my head instinctively, and as I looked up, something even more extraordinary happened. I saw shimmering sparkles dancing in the air right above my head. They glistened and sparkled for a few fleeting moments before vanishing as mysteriously as they had appeared.

Right after that, an overwhelming wave of love, peace, and acceptance washed over me. It felt as though I had been lifted from the ordinary world and embraced by a profound, otherworldly presence. My body was completely renewed, every cell vibrating with the purest frequency of love.

Then, I felt an incredible euphoria, an unbounded joy that made me feel as though I could soar through my room. The sensation was so exhilarating that it seemed like I was floating, unburdened by any earthly constraints. This unparalleled peace and joy were unlike anything I had ever felt before. It was a deep, soulful tranquility that touched the very core of my being, filling me with an overwhelming sense of divine love and embrace.

The power that surged through me was nothing short of glorious. It wasn't a fleeting sensation; it was a powerful, life-altering force that flowed through every fiber of my being. I could physically feel the intensity of the Holy Spirit's presence—its divine, tangible glory moving through me, filling me with an unshakable sense of purpose and a deep connection to everyone and everything around me. God's presence filled the entire room, so palpable I felt as though I could touch it in the air. It was serenity and joy beyond anything I had ever imagined. The experience was very peaceful and deeply spiritual, a clear manifestation of the Holy Spirit's divine essence.

This moment of divine interaction was not just a physical sensation but a deep spiritual revelation. The Holy Spirit had filled me with an overwhelming sense of presence and love, breaking through the limits of my physical and emotional boundaries. It was an incredible affirmation of God's power and the profound reality of the Holy Spirit working within me. I never wanted this feeling to end. Suddenly, I couldn't stop repeating: 'Wow, wow, I'm so grateful, so grateful, thank you, thank you, thank you...' I am beyond grateful and humbled by this breathtaking encounter and the renewed sense of purpose it has instilled in me.

God has graciously revealed Himself to me in a way that defied any explanations, and I knew that my life would never be the same. From that point on, my faith took on an entirely new dimension, as I stepped into a realm of spiritual vitality and divine glory.

This sense of awe was amplified even more when I later found out that another believer had encountered something strikingly similar to what I had experienced. Their description of the event—**word for word**—served as a powerful confirmation of the divine nature of what I had felt and seen. It became clear that my experience was not just a personal moment, but a profound encounter with the Holy Spirit. It affirmed that the Spirit's presence and work go beyond individual experiences and are part of a much greater, heavenly purpose. I realized that the greatest gift God had given me was salvation through His Holy Spirit—the glorious presence of God within saved believers—an unimaginable treasure that continues to shape my life.

And the best part about all of this is that when even one person comes to Christ and is saved, all of heaven rejoices. As Jesus Himself said in Luke 15:10, **"In the same way, I tell you, there is rejoicing in the presence of the angels of God over one sinner who repents."** The celebration in heaven is not just a quiet acknowledgment but a jubilant celebration—angels singing and all of heaven rejoicing over the salvation of each soul. This truth fills me with awe and gratitude, knowing that the moment a person turns to Christ, they are met not only with divine love but with a heavenly chorus of praise! Wow! What a tremendous honor!

I did nothing in my life to deserve such a revelation of the LORD. Nothing at all. This grace is too priceless, too magnificent. So I found myself asking, "Why me, God? Why?" In the stillness of my heart, I was overwhelmed by the weight of my past, unworthy of such a profound, life-altering experience. It wasn't until later that I discovered the truth: this divine encounter wasn't about me at all—it was about His love, His grace, and His desire to draw the humble and contrite heart near to Him. It's not about our merits or achievements; it's about our willingness to surrender—to open our hearts and seek a connection with the Divine. The precious Holy Spirit is accessible to all who genuinely humble themselves before God.

This realization changed everything for me. I discovered that God's Grace is not reserved for the perfect but is a gift for the willing. Let's be honest—none of us deserve this Grace. Divine Grace and mercy are unmerited, beyond anything we could ever earn. Yet, Jesus made us worthy and acceptable to God—only through His sacrifice, through the blood He shed on the cross, were we made worthy in Him. I came to understand that

grace isn't about striving to earn God's favor; it's about humbly receiving His unmerited love.

As this truth took a deep root in my heart, I was struck by the overwhelming joy of God's Spirit. The magnitude of that encounter left an indelible mark on my soul, filling me with joy, peace, and love I had never known before. It was the very presence of God that had come to dwell within me, igniting a fire of reverence and awe that I couldn't contain. This divine moment revealed the transformative power of the Holy Spirit in ways I could not have anticipated—God Himself, living in me. The peace I felt surpassed all understanding, and the love was overwhelming, like nothing I had ever experienced. It was as if the Creator of the Universe had wrapped me in His arms and whispered, "You are mine, and I AM yours." This was no ordinary encounter; it was a holy, sacred moment that left me forever changed. The Holy Spirit filled every part of me, and I knew in that instant that I would never be the same.

My beloved, I've just shared with you the unforgettable moment when I was filled with the Holy Spirit—and let me tell you, when it happens, you *know* it, **100 percent**. There's no second-guessing, no wondering if you missed a memo from Heaven. Nope! When you're saved by the Grace of God and filled with His Spirit, it comes with supernatural signs, wonders, and a spiritual glow-up that no skincare routine can compete with. It's a package deal, so to speak.

And here's the wild part: you won't be able to keep quiet about it. I mean it. Suddenly, you go from "I'm shy and terrified of what people think" to "Let me tell you what God did for me—in detail, with hand gestures and zero hesitation! All you want to do is talk about Jesus—every day, all day, 24/7. No breaks, no shame! Small talk becomes... well, small. Weather? Meh. Sports? Maybe later. But God? Oh yes, let's talk about Him again and again, and then once more for good measure. You find yourself completely captivated—like you've developed a holy obsession—and cannot get enough of God and His miracles. Of course, it's not coming from you—it's all the Holy Spirit igniting your very soul!

This moment isn't just a memory; it's a launchpad. It marked the beginning of my holy adventure with God, opening the door to miracles, rapid-fire spiritual growth, and the kind of joy that makes people wonder what you're drinking (spoiler: it's Living Water).

It's only when the Holy Spirit fills you that the supernatural journey really kicks into gear. We're talking about a full-blown, Holy-Spirit-fueled transformation. Suddenly, you're walking through life with divine GPS—turn-by-turn directions, straight from Heaven. The Holy Spirit starts handing out wisdom like candy on harvest night. He comforts you, convicts you, and somehow always knows when you need a spiritual nudge (or a holy shove). What begins with simple acts of surrender and repentance quickly unfolds into divine fireworks—healing, freedom, revelation, and moments so full of God's presence that you don't know whether to cry, laugh, or do both at the same time.

Within just seven months of surrendering my life to Christ, I experienced complete healing from depression, suicidal thoughts, chronic pain, and multiple addictions—yes, the whole bundle that had been dragging me down for years. These weren't just emotional boosts or motivational highs; they were supernatural breakthroughs. I had been desperate for change, truly desperate. And God? He showed up, rolled up His sleeves (figuratively speaking), and got to work. My hunger for real growth was met with His overwhelming Grace. I needed help, and He didn't just meet me halfway— He carried me the rest of the way like a Shepherd scooping up a sheep that wandered face-first into a bush.

After I was filled with the Holy Spirit, everything changed. This wasn't a lighthearted decision or a feel-good moment; it was the start of a whole new life—powered by the actual presence of God living inside me. The Spirit didn't just confirm my salvation; He activated something inside me that had been dormant my entire life. That healing I mentioned? It was no fluke. It was the direct result of divine intervention. God turned my hopelessness into hope, my pain into peace, and my mess into a message. And now, I walk through each day not just as someone who believes in God, but as someone who has *met* Him—and is still being transformed by Him.

This journey began the moment I said Yes to Jesus—but it's far from over. If anything, it feels like I'm still just getting started. And I know—without a doubt—that the best is yet to come.

Chapter 5

Salvation is Simple: Ask, Seek, Knock

Shortly after being filled with God's Holy Spirit, I received another powerful confirmation from Jesus' gentle voice saying, "Seek"—a clear and unmistakable encouragement to continue seeking Him without hesitation. The moment was so surreal, filled with assurance that He was present, actively awakening me to a new reality and an exciting, fresh beginning in my life. That one word—"Seek"—stayed with me and stirred something deep in my heart. I didn't fully understand it at the time, but I knew it was important.

Later, in my journey of salvation, I stumbled upon Bible verses related to this very word, and what I discovered left me speechless. In Luke 11:9-13, Jesus Himself gives us clear and invaluable instructions on how to receive salvation. These instructions are the same for everyone—something I wasn't aware of at the time, since I had never read the Bible before my salvation. I owe a great deal of gratitude to my grandmother, who did read the Bible and passed down this treasure to me! Here's what Jesus says in those verses:

"So I say to you: Ask and it will be given to you; seek and you will find; knock and the door will be opened to you. For everyone who asks receives; the one who seeks finds; and to the one who knocks, the door will be opened. Which of you fathers, if your son asks for a fish, will give him a snake instead? Or if he asks for an egg,

will give him a scorpion? If you then, though you are evil, know how to give good gifts to your children, how much more will Your Father in heaven *give the Holy Spirit to those who ask Him!"*

Jesus uses the analogy of earthly fathers, who, despite their flaws, still desire to give good gifts to their children. How much more, then, will our Holy Heavenly Father respond generously when we ask for His Holy Spirit?!

This passage holds a profound and simple key, a simple formula to salvation: we just have to ask. **Ask for the Holy Spirit**, sincerely and persistently after saying the LORD's prayer. Wholeheartedly. Could it truly be that simple? Yes! Salvation is an incredible gift, freely given to all who earnestly ask, seek, and knock. In response, He blesses us with His most precious gift—the Holy Spirit. He is also known as the Spirit of Christ, the LORD's Spirit, God's Spirit, the Comforter, the Spirit of Truth, just to name a few. The Holy Spirit is the active presence of God in the world today, transforming, empowering, guiding, teaching, protecting, and comforting those who are truly saved.

God desires to give us the Holy Spirit, along with the assurance of salvation and the power to live a transformed life. This invitation is open to everyone who repents by saying the LORD's prayer and asks God for the Holy Spirit. As mentioned earlier in Chapter 3, these are the easy steps to receiving this holy gift. **"How much more will Your Father in heaven give the Holy Spirit to those who ask Him!"** My friends, why not give it a try—what do you have to lose?

My grandmother was right all along when she taught me the LORD's Prayer as a child, especially the part about the plea for the Holy Spirit. Looking back, I now realize that the

Holy Spirit led her to share those instructions with me, knowing it would lead to my salvation one day. It wasn't by chance that she introduced me to this treasure so early; God, in His perfect timing was planting the seeds of faith in my heart. In my moments of desperation as an adult, that prayer was the first thing that came to mind, reminding me of His presence and divine nature. It was through Him that I found salvation, the peace, and the love I had been searching for all along. And now, I realize it was all part of God's divine plan, guiding me toward the moment of salvation. I can take no credit for this journey, for it is by His grace alone that I am saved, and I give Him all the glory for the work He has been doing in my life through His Holy Spirit.

When I think about the role my grandmother played in my life, I'm reminded of the truth found in Romans 10:14-15—a powerful passage that speaks to the importance of those who bring the message of salvation: **"How then will they call on Him to save them unless they believe in Him? And how can they believe in Him if they have never heard about Him? And how can they hear about Him unless someone tells them? And how will anyone go and tell them without being sent by the LORD? That is why the Scriptures say, 'How beautiful are the feet of messengers who bring good news!'"** (Romans 10:14-15, NLT).

These verses show us that, for salvation to be possible, someone must share the message, and I believe my grandmother's role in making me memorize the LORD's prayer was a part of that divine plan—she was one of the messengers sent to help me be saved today. God placed in her the desire to teach me this prayer and plea for the Holy Spirit, knowing it would lead to my salvation today. Just as Romans 10:15 declares, **'How beautiful are the feet of**

messengers who bring good news!' I see now that my grandmother was one of those messengers, sent by God to help me hear and believe the truth that led to my salvation. Hallelujah! Praise the LORD!

As Jesus further confirms this in John 6:44, **"No one can come to Me unless the Father Who sent Me draws them, and I will raise them up at the last day."** And in Jeremiah 29:12-13, **"Then you will call on Me and come and pray to Me, and I will listen to you. You will seek Me and find Me when you seek Me with all your heart."** Additionally, in Revelation 3:20, Jesus says, **"Here I AM! I stand at the door and knock. If anyone hears My voice and opens the door, I will come in and eat with that person, and they with Me."** These verses teach us that God is constantly pursuing us, drawing us near, and inviting us to experience His love and salvation. The door is here—Jesus is that very door! Knock, and it will be opened to you.

These passages beautifully echo God's promise that He will be found by those who earnestly seek Him, and they perfectly align with my own journey. When I turned to God with all my heart—broken, imperfect, and full of sin—I not only encountered His presence but also received His forgiveness and complete acceptance. It's another affirmation that is both deeply personal and universally true—one that resonates with anyone who has ever reached out to God in faith, seeking Him wholeheartedly.

Together, these verses, along with others throughout Scriptures, paint a beautiful picture of God's openness and faithfulness to those who seek Him. The consistent message in the Bible is very clear: when we earnestly seek God with our whole hearts, He will allow us to find Him. The more we seek Him, the more we experience His presence in our lives—this remains true even after we are saved. As we immerse ourselves in His sacred Word and prayer, continually seeking His presence, we encounter His love for us in deeper ways. But seeking God isn't just something we do once—it's the very heart of receiving and living out our salvation.

Salvation is **not** a one-time, "say a prayer, and you're saved" kind of thing. It's not about praying the LORD's Prayer once and being done with it. It's not like that at all! Receiving the gift of salvation is a **continual act of pursuing God wholeheartedly—praying earnestly and pleading until you receive His salvation.** God knows the intentions of our hearts. God desires to see our humbleness, our genuine hunger for Him and His truth. He wants to see how much we truly desire His salvation. We need to keep pressing, keep asking, keep praying—praying the LORD's Prayer with sincerity and persistence.

I spent over a year in persistent prayer—genuinely sorrowful for my sins and continually pleading with God for the gift of the Holy Spirit. As I mentioned earlier, I wasn't raised in a religious environment, so I didn't realize at the time that what I was doing was actually an act of repentance. I was simply pouring my heart out to God, unaware that this was exactly what He was looking for all along.

At the lowest point of my life—at the end of myself— alone, broken, and tormented by thoughts I couldn't explain, I was led to seek comfort in prayer. It's in those moments of desperation—when you feel you've reached your limit but still persist in knocking on Heaven's door—that God reveals His love and grace in the most powerful ways. You need to keep pleading with God until His peace and acceptance overflow your heart, and His presence becomes a daily reality in your life.

Still, it took me over a year to receive this blessing. For others, it may happen sooner. It's not about the timeline—it's about how earnestly, how sincerely, and how consistently you're willing to seek the truth and invite the Holy Spirit to fill the emptiness inside. It's not even the intensity of your crying that matters—it's the sincerity of your heart. That is what truly matters to God—the authenticity of your repentance.

Are you truly hungry for answers—for the truth about whether Jesus Christ is real? Are you willing to find out if the salvation He offers—and the gift of the Holy Spirit—isn't just a fairy tale, but could become your reality too?

My dear friends, may God's mercy and grace reach you swiftly, and may He bless you with His salvation even sooner than I received it. In the name of our LORD Jesus Christ, I plead this. Amen.

In Elevation Worship's song **"Trust in God,"** the lyrics proclaim, "I sought the LORD, and He heard, and He answered. That's why I trust Him." Those words say it all! This powerful declaration of faith perfectly captures the incredible experience of seeking God and feeling the awe of receiving His response. I can't help but feel this song resonates deeply with me, as it mirrors my own encounter with the Divine. For anyone who has ever reached out to God in their moments of need, these lyrics hit home. They are far more than just words—they are a living testament to God's unwavering faithfulness.

I, too, have sought God in my times of need, and to my

amazement, He heard me! He answered me! This song doesn't just speak to my heart; it shouts out the truth of what happens when you reach out to God and encounter His faithfulness firsthand. This is why I trust Him—because I know He is real, and He is waiting to answer you, too. Don't wait for God to drive you into His arms—seek Him now, while there is still time. God is ready to reveal Himself in ways that will leave you in awe, and He promises to hear you when you call. Trust me, He's just waiting for you to reach out!

Isn't it amazing that such an eternal truth is so accessible? The simplicity of salvation is nothing short of astonishing! It's for anyone willing to seek, ask, and knock—just as Jesus promised. The idea that God responds to our sincere requests and desires to give us good things—especially His Holy Spirit—may seem surprisingly accessible, yet many people overlook or are unaware of it at all, just like I was. This confirms that God made salvation so accessible because of His immense love and mercy for us. His love is sacrificial, reaching out to every one of us, regardless of our past or background.

God's love reaches us even when we have no idea He's there. I, too, had no real awareness of God's presence in my life until that moment when, in my brokenness, I reached out with perseverance and a sincere heart. I asked, and He answered in ways I never thought possible. This just goes to show that salvation is not reserved for the "religious" or those with deep theological knowledge. As Jesus Himself spoke in Matthew 11:25 (NIV): **"I praise You, Father, LORD of heaven and earth, because You have hidden these things from the wise and learned, and revealed them to *little children*."** Here, Jesus acknowledges how the

53

wisdom of the world often prevents people from grasping the truth of God's love. In a way, God chooses to reveal Himself to those who are humble and open-hearted, not necessarily to the religious or the learned.

This theme is not unique to Jesus' words—it's echoed throughout Scripture. The prophet Isaiah 29:14 (NIV) also says: **"Therefore once more I will astound these people with wonder upon wonder; the wisdom of the wise will perish, the intelligence of the intelligent will vanish."** The wisdom that the world holds so dear will ultimately fade away. What the world considers wise, God will expose as foolishness. He has a way of surprising us, often choosing to confound the wisdom of the world with the simplicity of His truth.

The prophet Jeremiah continues this same message, further emphasizing the contrast between worldly wisdom and God's truth. In Jeremiah 8:9 (NIV), it is written: **"The wise will be put to shame; they will be dismayed and trapped. Since they have rejected the Word of the LORD, what kind of wisdom do they have?"** Those who reject God's Word may appear wise in the eyes of the world, but their wisdom is ultimately empty—unable to grasp the deeper truths of God. The LORD's wisdom is eternal and far beyond human understanding.

The Apostle Paul ties all of this together in the New Testament. In 1 Corinthians 1:19-21 (NIV), it says: **"For it is written: I will destroy the wisdom of the wise; the intelligence of the intelligent I will frustrate.' Where is the wise person? Where is the teacher of the law? Where is the philosopher of this age? Has not God made foolish the wisdom of the world? For since in the wisdom of**

God the world through its wisdom did not know Him, God was pleased through the foolishness of what was preached to save those who believe." Here, Paul emphasizes that the world's wisdom, in all its intellect and pride, is insufficient to comprehend God. His wisdom works in ways that appear foolish to the world, yet it is through this "foolishness" that God saves those who have faith.

This brings us to a common misconception: the belief that all priests, pastors, or individuals in leadership roles within the church are automatically saved and, thus, filled with the Holy Spirit simply because of their involvement in ministry. However, this is far from the truth, and it is more common than many realize. Just as in biblical times, the Pharisees—Jewish religious leaders who were teachers of the law—considered themselves righteous and believed they had no need for repentance or God's grace. They believed they were already righteous in God's eyes, which led to their arrogance and a tendency to look down on others. Not much has changed since then, has it?

God desires repentance, **not** self-righteousness, and He calls everyone to turn to Him, as confirmed in Acts 17:30 (ESV), which states: **"The times of ignorance God overlooked, but now He commands all people everywhere to repent."** The Bible is explicit that salvation is a matter of the heart, not one's position, accomplishments, title, or role. It is available only to those who humbly repent and accept God's grace.

A pastor or priest, just like anyone else, **must recognize** their need for salvation and repent of their sins before God in order to be saved. We cannot receive mercy if we do not believe we need it. As Romans 10:9-10 (CEV) states: **"So you will be saved if you honestly say, 'Jesus is LORD,' and if** you believe with all your heart that God raised Him from death. God will accept you and save you, if you truly believe this and tell it to others." This is a personal confession of faith, not one that is done for you by your position in the church.

Moreover, Matthew 7:21-23 provides a powerful lesson: simply doing good works or serving in ministry does **not** guarantee salvation. Jesus says, **"Not everyone who says to me, 'LORD, LORD,' will enter the Kingdom of Heaven, but only the one who does the will of My Father Who is in Heaven. Many will say to Me on that day, 'LORD, LORD, did we not prophesy in Your name, and in Your name drive out demons and in Your name perform many miracles?' Then I will tell them plainly, 'I never knew you. Away from Me, you evildoers!'"**

In this passage, Jesus is warning that outward religious actions—even miraculous ones like prophesying, casting out demons, and performing mighty works—are not enough to enter the Kingdom of Heaven. When Jesus says, **"I never knew you. Away from Me, you evildoers,"** He's speaking to people who used His name and performed impressive works, but whose hearts were far from Him. They had selfish motives in their hearts, seeking power, fame, money, recognition, or personal gain—but none of these can grant salvation. God sees the hidden motives in our hearts; nothing is hidden from Him. What truly saves us is genuine repentance and belief in the words we speak—especially when we pray the LORD's Prayer and ask for the Holy Spirit.

So, yes, even priests and pastors must humble themselves before God Almighty and fully repent, believe in Jesus Christ, and receive Him as their Savior in order to be saved and filled with the Holy Spirit. Just like anyone else, their salvation depends on repentance, not on their title, accomplishments, or role. John 3:5 confirms that to enter the Kingdom of God, one must be "born again"—a personal transformation that only comes from being filled with the Holy Spirit: **"Jesus answered, 'Very truly I tell you, no one can enter the Kingdom of God unless they are born of water and the Spirit.'"**

This transformation is directly connected to repentance, as Acts 2:38 emphasizes: **"Peter replied, 'Repent and be baptized, every one of you, in the name of Jesus Christ for the forgiveness of your sins. And you will receive the gift of the Holy Spirit.'"** John 3:18 (NIV) further clarifies, **"Whoever believes in Him (Jesus) is not condemned, but whoever does not believe stands condemned already because they have not believed in the name of God's One and only Son."**

Consequently, titles, roles, accomplishments, or positions within the church—or anywhere else—do not guarantee salvation. This truth applies to all of us. True salvation comes through genuine faith and repentance, not through one's works or personal beliefs about how good we are.

Our good works—or thinking that just being a good person is enough to be saved—represents the greatest lie the devil tells. Good deeds, such as charity, giving money to the church, or living a morally upright life, are important and should be done as an outpouring of our faith. However, these actions in and of themselves will not guarantee our place in heaven.

Let me emphasize this again: we are not saved by our good deeds or by simply believing we're good enough to go to heaven after we pass away. While it's important to live with integrity, generosity, and love, salvation is not earned through good works—it's a gift from God.

At the end of the day, we tend to compare ourselves to one another, but that's not the standard we should be measuring ourselves against. Instead, we should compare ourselves to the holiness and perfection of God, and by that measure, none of us can claim to be "good." The Bible is explicit about this: **"No one is righteous, not even one"** (Romans 3:10). Jesus Himself said in Mark 10:18, **"Why do you call Me good? No one is good—except God alone."** The truth is, our salvation is not based on what we do but on what Jesus did for us on the cross. No one can earn salvation through their own goodness or accomplishments, because it is only by God's grace that we are saved, not by our own efforts.

Therefore, while we are called to do good works after receiving salvation—works that reflect the transformation in our hearts through Christ—they do not save us. Good works are a response to God's love and grace, not a way to earn favor or a ticket to heaven. The Word of God makes this clear: salvation is a gift we receive through faith in Jesus Christ alone, and this is why repentance and belief in the work of Jesus on the cross are essential.

Did you know that God's Word says, **"But I tell you that anyone who looks at a woman lustfully has already committed adultery with her in his heart"** (Matthew 5:28, NIV)? That means if anyone, regardless of gender, looks with lust at someone they're not married to, they've committed a serious sin in their heart. This sin is so severe that it separates us from God and deserves eternal punishment. This is just one example of how our Holy God views us in our natural state. Even something as seemingly small as one curse word is disgusting to God because He is **holy**, and there is **no darkness in Him at all** (1 John 1:5). He is pure and perfect, and we fall short of that holiness in every way.

The Bible is crystal clear that no one can perfectly obey God's Commandments, not even for a single day. This is because the Law doesn't just look at our outward actions but also judges our thoughts, which come from our hearts. Our thoughts reveal the true condition of our hearts, which is the true indicator of our righteousness—or lack thereof—in God's eyes. Do you have pure thoughts every second of every day? The Ten Commandments, which were given by God to guide us, could never save us—so what makes us think our own efforts could?

God is holy, and He requires holiness. But the only way we could be made holy was through **His intervention. He had to sacrifice Himself on the cross** to redeem us from sin and eternal punishment. Christ rescued us from the curse of the Law when He became a curse in our place (Galatians 3:13). Through His death and resurrection, we are offered the Holy Spirit, who works within us to transform us into the image of Christ (Romans 8:29). **Only His Holy Spirit** can accomplish this **supernatural perfection** in us. We can't do it ourselves.

Now, do you still think you are a good person when compared to the holiness of our Almighty Creator? Scripture is consistent on this: **"for all have sinned and fall short of** the glory of God" (Romans 3:23). No one can come close to the perfection of God. No one on their own.

God does not want to live among wicked and rebellious people in Heaven, so He had to make a way for us to be made new. The good news is that Jesus has already made that way through His sacrifice. **"Therefore, if anyone is in Christ, the new creation has come: The old has gone, the new is here!"** (2 Corinthians 5:17). It is through this new birth, through the indwelling of the Holy Spirit, that we can live lives pleasing to God. We can't achieve this transformation on our own, but by grace through faith in Jesus Christ, we can be made new, be made holy, and receive the gift of eternal life.

This is why the good news is so out of this world—literally! The Bible tells us that, despite our failures, Jesus came to offer us a new way—a **New Covenant of Grace**, founded **not** on rigid rules and legalism but on the unmerited grace of God (Romans 6:14). The New Covenant of Grace represents the fresh work of God through Christ, signaling the spiritual transformation of our hearts by the power of the Holy Spirit. It invites us to embrace the supernatural transformation that only God can bring, calling us to accept change, growth, and renewal in Christ.

You see, humanity could never meet God's perfect standard under the old legalistic covenant, which is why Jesus had to come as God incarnate. As the perfect sacrifice for our sins, He offered us salvation through repentance and belief in His work on the cross. Jesus Himself declared, **"It is finished"** (John 19:30), meaning He completed the work necessary for our redemption. We are now free from the law, and through His grace, we are made righteous. In Christ, the demands of the law are fulfilled, and righteousness is granted through faith in Him alone. In other words, Jesus perfectly fulfilled the law, bringing it to its intended purpose, so that now righteousness comes not from obeying the law, but through repentance and faith in Him alone.

Now, we must realize that we can't save ourselves through the law and that we need a Savior. Jesus Himself preached, **"Repent, for the Kingdom of Heaven has come near"** (Matthew 4:17). True repentance means acknowledging our inability to meet God's holiness and recognizing our need for His mercy and grace. It's a call to turn to Him for forgiveness, knowing that we can't achieve salvation by our own efforts.

Once again, salvation doesn't come from our good deeds or from believing we are good enough; it comes from recognizing our need for a Savior and accepting God's gift of grace—His Holy Spirit. As Ephesians 2:4-9 (NIV) says, **"But because of His great love for us, God, Who is rich in mercy, made us alive with Christ even when we were dead in transgressions—it is by grace you have been saved. And God raised us up with Christ and seated us with Him in the heavenly realms in Christ Jesus, in order that in the coming ages He might show the incomparable riches of His grace, expressed in His kindness to us in Christ Jesus. For it is by grace you have been saved, through faith—and this is not from yourselves, it is the gift of God—not by works, so that no one can boast."** See, it's a precious gift from our Triune God, emphasizing that our salvation is entirely His work. This means there is no room for boasting or pride in our own accomplishments; all glory belongs to God, who freely offers us the gift of eternal life in heaven *after* we repent, of course.

Romans 11:6 (NIV) further emphasizes this: **"And if by grace, then it is no longer by works; if it were, grace would no longer be grace."** This verse beautifully confirms that salvation is entirely based on God's grace and not anything we can achieve through our actions. Our salvation is a gift, not something we can earn through works. The moment we try to earn it, we completely nullify grace. It is purely God's unmerited favor that saves us.

So, the question now is: Are you ready to accept this gift of grace? Have you recognized that you need a Savior, and that Jesus is the only way? **"Jesus answered, 'I AM the way and the truth and the life. No one comes to the Father except through Me'"** (John 14:6).

We are saved *only* by what Jesus Christ did for us on the cross—His perfect, sinless life, His willing suffering, His shed blood, His sacrifice, and His resurrection, which **made it possible** for God to send us His Holy Spirit. We rely on what Jesus accomplished on the cross, not on anything we can do to earn favor. His work on the cross is complete; it is finished. It's fully paid for all of our sins—past, present, and future. We rest in His finished work, not in trying to "earn" salvation. This is the foundation of God's salvation. It is only through His Divine Grace that we are saved. **Jesus Christ is our Grace!** Salvation itself is simple; it's not meant to be complicated. Yet, people often complicate it. Religion complicates it. And the enemy delights in confusing us about this simple truth.

Let me further clarify this distinction that many new believers often confuse after reading the Bible: the difference between the works God speaks of *after* we are saved and the misconception that these works are necessary for salvation.

The Bible plainly teaches that we are called to do good works, but these works are not the means of our salvation. Rather, they are the natural outcome of salvation—a response to God's love and grace, **empowered by the Holy Spirit Himself**. Once we are saved, the Holy Spirit works within us to transform our hearts and lives, leading us to do good works, for it is God who works in us to will and to act in order to fulfill His good purpose (Philippians 2:13, NIV).

In fact, the Bible explains the good works we are called to do *after* we are saved. In Ephesians 2:10 (AMP), it says, **"For we are His workmanship, [His] master work, a work of art, created in Christ Jesus, reborn from above— spiritually transformed, renewed, ready to be used for good works, which God prepared for us beforehand, taking paths which He set so that we would walk in them [living the good life which He prearranged and made ready for us]."** This means that the good works God calls us to do come *after* we are saved and filled with the Holy Spirit. These works are not about what we think we should do, but rather what God has already prepared for us to do long ago. They are not about following our own will, but about fulfilling God's will.

Jesus affirms this truth in John 14:12 (NIV), declaring that those who believe in Him and walk in alignment with His will are empowered to do extraordinary things: **"Very truly I tell you, whoever believes in Me will do the works I have been doing, and they will do even greater things than these, because I AM going to the Father."** This shows us that, through His power, we are called to live out the works He has prepared for us—not only the things He did, but even greater things!

Jesus further emphasized this in His final instructions to the disciples. In Mark 16:15–18 (NIV), He said: **"Go into all the world and preach the Gospel to all creation. Whoever believes and is baptized will be saved, but whoever does not believe will be condemned. And these signs will accompany those who believe: In My Name they will drive out demons; they will speak in new tongues; they will pick up snakes with their hands; and when they drink deadly poison, it will not hurt them at all; they will place their hands on sick people, and they will get well."**

And in Luke 24:47–48 (NIV), He declared, **"Repentance for the forgiveness of sins will be preached in His name to all nations, beginning at Jerusalem. You are witnesses of these things."** These verses make it unmistakably clear: the works of preaching the gospel, healing the sick, casting out demons, and operating in spiritual authority are not limited to the original apostles or early church leaders. As Jesus said in the verse above—Mark 16:17—**"These signs will accompany those who believe,"** meaning *anyone* who places their faith in Him. This includes ordinary people in every generation, from every background, in every part of the world. These works are meant to continue through all believers who are filled with the Holy Spirit—not just pastors, missionaries, or church elders, but *every* Spirit-filled follower of Christ.

This divine empowerment is not reserved for a select few—it extends to every believer, including you and me, today. When Jesus ascended, He made way for the Holy Spirit to be poured out, so that we could be filled with God's power to fulfill His will on the earth. We are now part of the ongoing mission of God, walking in the same authority and calling He gave to the early church.

As we embrace this calling, it's important to remember that these works are not a way to earn God's favor; rather, they are the natural outflow of a heart transformed by the Holy Spirit. When we are filled with His Spirit, we are not only given the desire to do God's will—we are also empowered to carry it out. Through His guidance, we allow Him to work through us in our everyday actions, fulfilling His purpose for our lives. The good works we walk in are not accidental—they are intentional, God-ordained, and spiritually empowered.

Therefore, it is both a joyful responsibility and a tremendous privilege for every believer—not just the spiritually elite—to seek God in prayer, asking Him to reveal the specific works He has prepared for us. As we walk by faith, led by the Holy Spirit, we step into the same power and purpose that fueled the early church. We are living proof that God's mission continues through ordinary people doing extraordinary things—because of an extraordinary God who now lives and works through us.

To summarize, salvation is a free gift of grace, received through genuine repentance and faith in receiving Spirit of Christ. Good works come afterward, not as a requirement for salvation, but as the natural fruit of salvation. The Holy Spirit empowers us to do these works, and they serve as a natural response of gratitude for the amazing grace and the promise of eternal life we receive through salvation. It's crucial to get this distinction right, as it helps us to understand that we cannot work our way into salvation, but we are called to live in a way that reflects the salvation we have already received.

As you embark on this incredible journey of salvation, remember that it is through grace alone that we are saved, not by our good deeds or accomplishments. Jesus has made the way clear for us, and all we need to do is earnestly seek Him with all our hearts. Just as He promised, when we ask, seek, and knock, He will answer. It's not about perfection—it's about genuine repentance, faith in Him, and a heart open to His transformative work. The Holy Spirit is the gift God desires to give to all who come to Him, and once we receive Him, we are empowered to live a life full of purpose and grace. Don't complicate this simple truth; salvation is within your reach right now. The instructions are here—grab it, hold it tight, and never let go. God is waiting to meet you in ways beyond your wildest dreams! Be humble, patient, and persistent in your pursuit. He is worth the wait!

Chapter 6

The Living Word: From Fairy Tales to Divine Truth

Shortly after being filled with the Holy Spirit, a friend gifted me a Bible—a coincidence, or so I thought at the time. I had never read the Bible before and, like many, believed it was just a collection of fairy tales and made-up stories. I had convinced myself that it was irrelevant to today's world, claiming its message had been lost through countless translations and its ancient origins. I doubted its authenticity and thought it held no bearing on my life. Little did I know that many prophecies in the Bible had already been fulfilled, profoundly shaping the course of history. Now I realize how wrong I had been—those thoughts were lies from the enemy, meant to keep me from the life-changing power of God's Word. The Bible is not only relevant; it is timeless, speaking directly to our hearts. At the time, I couldn't have known that this book I had once dismissed would soon become the living source of truth and transformation in my life.

My friend suggested I start with the New Testament, beginning with the story of Jesus as the perfect sacrifice for our sins, which established the New Covenant of Grace. Reading with fresh eyes and an open heart, I was struck by many apparent coincidences that seemed to resonate with my own experiences. It became clear that the Bible was not just a book, but a living testament to God's boundless love, guidance, and truth. It was as if each page was infused with the breath of life, pulsing with meaning and purpose. One moment stands out vividly: as I read, I experienced something I can hardly describe; the letters began to lift off the pages, rising before me. It wasn't a trick of the light, nor was it simply my imagination—this truly happened. The words were not just ink on paper; they were alive, tangible, and as real as the air we breathe. Later, this unexplainable phenomenon was even confirmed by other believers who had experienced similar encounter after their salvation.

In that sacred moment, it became abundantly clear to me: God's Word is alive. It is not bound by time or circumstance, but eternally relevant, speaking to the hearts of all who seek His truth. Each page spoke to me personally, revealing God's infinite wisdom and His deep, unwavering longing to reconcile and transform His people into the image of His Son, Jesus Christ. His sacred Word has the power to change us from within! I marveled at how timeless and living the Scriptures are—how they reach into the depths of my soul, drawing me closer to the Creator, and guiding me on a path of restoration and hope. It was more than just reading; it was an encounter with the living God, a reminder that His Word will never return void, but will accomplish the work He intended. I stood in awe, realizing that I was not merely learning about God, but experiencing His power in every word.

In my journey through the sacred Scriptures, I came to a profound realization: Jesus Christ is the very Word made Flesh, coming to dwell among us. As the Gospel of John declares, Jesus is the eternal Word of God who took on human flesh. John 1:1 (NKJV) says, **"In the beginning was the Word, and the Word was with God, and the Word was God."** Then, John 1:14 (NKJV) affirms this astounding truth: **"And the Word became flesh and dwelt among us..."** Jesus, the incarnate Word, is God Himself—revealed in human form, living out God's perfect will and showing us the way to true life. Through Him, the Word became tangible—accessible to humanity in a way that transcended mere text or doctrine. He is not just a messenger of the Word, but the Word Himself, the ultimate expression of God's truth.

Jesus, as the Word made flesh, draws us into His love by calling us to embrace His teachings and live them out—because only then can we experience the freedom His truth brings. The Bible became more than just words on a page—it transformed into a living dialogue, a sacred communication between me and the Creator of the universe. As I read, I felt my mind being renewed, my thoughts becoming clearer and less clouded by darkness, and my heart being purified in a way that could only be described as supernatural.

I came to understand that **His Word has the supernatural power to cleanse us from within**, purifying our hearts and minds as we engage with it daily. By receiving God's sacred knowledge and truth, a **deep and lasting change** begins to take root. This knowledge has the power to purify our minds and hearts, renewing us from the inside out. As we absorb the truth, it shifts our perspective, aligning our thoughts with His will. This awareness of the truth doesn't just inform us—it automatically starts to change us from within. With this understanding, we are no longer the same; we are continually being made new.

The Apostle Paul writes in Romans 12:2 (NIV), **"Do not conform to the pattern of this world, but be transformed by the renewing of your mind. Then you will be able to test and approve what God's will is—His good, pleasing and perfect will."** When we embrace God's truth, it renews our minds, and through this renewal, we are conformed to the image of Christ. It became evident that the Scriptures

69

were not just ancient writings, but a continual process of cleansing, purifying, and making us holy—shaping us to reflect the holiness of Jesus Himself. Let me emphasize this once more: Through daily Bible reading, the Scriptures not only cleanse us but also sanctify us—making us holy, just as Jesus is holy. How incredible is that? There's nothing greater than God's supernatural transformative power!

I know that it's not always easy to begin reading the Bible. For many, diving into the Scriptures feels overwhelming—not just because of how vast they are, but also because of the spiritual opposition that constantly tries to keep us from reading them. Of course, they want to do everything in their power to stop you from accessing the truth that renews your mind and heart. They know that within the Word of God lies the power to transform your life, the secrets of God's Kingdom, and the wisdom that can set you free. The enemy's primary goal is to keep us ignorant of God's truth because he understands that once we grasp the full understanding of Scripture, we are empowered to stand firm against his attacks.

But it's not just about gaining intellectual knowledge; it's about truly understanding the authority we have in Jesus Christ. As we dive into the Word, we discover that we are not powerless in this spiritual battle. The Scriptures reveal our position in Christ, teaching us that, through His victory on the cross, we have been given real authority over the enemy and his attacks. **The Bible isn't a book of rules meant to restrict or control us—as many mistakenly believe—it's our spiritual armor, our training manual, and our lifeline.** It equips us, protects us, and empowers us to stand firm.

Jesus Himself said in John 8:32, **"Then you will know the truth, and the truth will set you free."** The truth not only sets us free but also equips us with spiritual authority to overcome the enemy's lies. The devil knows that when we fully embrace the authority we have in Christ, we are no longer his captives but empowered warriors in God's Kingdom.

In 2 Corinthians 4:4, Paul warns that **"the god of this age (satan) has blinded the minds of unbelievers, so that they cannot see the light of the Gospel that displays the glory of Christ, Who is the Image of God."** This tells us something crucial: there's a deliberate strategy to keep people spiritually blind. If satan can keep you away from the Bible, he can keep you believing lies. He can distort your identity, your purpose, and your view of God.

The devil fights so hard to keep us away from the Word of God—because he knows the power it holds to transform lives, expose his lies, and strengthen believers. Satan knows the Bible way too well—not to obey it, but to twist its meaning and use it against us. He did the same thing to Jesus in the wilderness (Matthew 4), quoting Scripture out of context in an attempt to tempt Him. And he still does this today, accusing us before God whenever we stumble or fall into sin. Revelation 12:10 calls him **"the accuser of our brothers and sisters,"** because he constantly looks for reasons to shame and condemn those who belong to God.

But Hebrews 4:12 teaches us of what the Word of God really is: **"alive and active. Sharper than any double-edged sword, it penetrates even to dividing soul and spirit, joints and marrow; it judges the thoughts and attitudes of the heart."**

The Bible is not just a book of ancient stories or religious rules—it is the living voice of God. It speaks directly to our hearts. When you read it, it reveals what's really going on inside of you—your hidden motives, your doubts, your wounds, and your need for healing. It teaches you how to recognize sin and turn away from it. It gives you wisdom when you're confused. It gives you peace when you're anxious. It reminds you of who you are in Christ when the enemy tries to bring shame. It tells you the truth when the world lies to you.

That's why spending time in the Word is so crucial—because it builds your faith, renews your mind, and prepares you to stand firm when life gets hard. And when you start declaring God's promises out loud, resisting temptation with Scripture (just like Jesus did), and living according to what God says, the enemy begins to lose his influence over you. The more you know the truth, the less power his lies will have.

This is exactly why he works overtime to make Bible reading feel difficult—through distractions, discouragement, or even exhaustion. He's terrified of what happens when you start walking in truth. The enemy fights hard because he knows the truth you're uncovering will break his hold on your life. But here's the good news: when you feel that resistance, it's a sign that you're heading in the right direction. So, keep pressing forward. As you seek God through His Word, you *will* experience the transformation and freedom He's promised.

I was once in that place too—hesitant to start reading the Bible and not fully understanding why I felt this resistance. I'd sit down with good intentions, and suddenly I'd feel like I

hadn't slept in three years. Or I'd finally get quiet time and—
ding!—a random text from an old friend I hadn't spoken to
since forever. Or suddenly I'd remember I absolutely *had* to
clean the junk drawer or reorganize my daughter's sock
collection. It was like everything in the universe conspired to
interrupt me. Getting through a chapter without distractions
felt like winning a gold medal in spiritual warfare. And
honestly, the enemy will likely try to distract you too—
whether it's while reading the Bible or **even this very
book**—because he knows the truth has the power to set you
free.

The way I overcame it was by simply praying to God,
asking Him to give me a **desire** for His Word and the
persistence to keep reading. And after praying that prayer a
few times, something amazing happened—I just couldn't
stop! It turned into a deep longing, a spiritual hunger to read,
and the more I read, the more I wanted to know. It was as if
God flipped a switch in my soul. The Bible came alive—
pages that once felt distant suddenly felt personal and deeply
relevant. It became part of me, like a spiritual nourishment I
couldn't go without. Even the genealogies, which I used to
skip over, began to fascinate me. That's the power of the
Holy Spirit—He doesn't just help us read the Word; He
makes us crave it, love it, and live it out. It became as
essential to me as my phone—always near, always speaking,
always guiding. But unlike a phone, it doesn't drain me; it fills
me.

For those just beginning their journey with the Bible, I
recommend starting with the **Holy Bible Channel** on
YouTube, or using the Audible app to listen to audio versions
like the **Holy Bible (NIV) read by David Suchet,** or **The
Word of Promise Audio Bible (NKJV)**. And if you prefer

a hard copy, I suggest starting with the NIV (New International Version)—it's an easier read for beginners while staying true to the original meaning. They're great starting points for anyone new to Scripture, and helpful tools for building a strong foundation in God's Word. Remember, the key is to ask God for desire and persistence. Don't be afraid to take that first step, and let God's Word begin to transform you just as it has been transforming me.

Once we receive the knowledge and truth of God's Word, we allow the Holy Spirit to work in us more powerfully and intimately. He helps us remember the teachings we've read and studied, bringing Bible verses to our minds exactly when we need them most. In moments of trial, confusion, or temptation, the Holy Spirit will bring to the forefront of our thoughts the promises, wisdom, and instructions of Scripture. This divine recall isn't something we can accomplish on our own—it's the work of the Holy Spirit within us. He ensures that God's Word isn't just another book we read and finish, but a source of divine teaching and instruction, woven into every part of our lives.

The transformation we experience isn't just a result of reading the Bible alone; it's the combination of God's truth and the ongoing work of the Holy Spirit who dwells within saved believers. This renewal is certain, but it is also slow and gradual. I often wish it were faster, that I could see more immediate change in myself, but I've learned that the slow process is necessary. It's in this slow and steady transformation that we are refined, shaped, and prepared for God's works. If the process were too quick, we might become prideful, thinking the change is something we've done on our own. But we must remember that this is not our work—it's the work of the Holy Spirit. It is God who promised long ago to transform us so that He could dwell among us in Heaven, and He is the one Who faithfully carries out this work in our lives. As we trust in God's timing and the Holy Spirit's work, we can be confident that this renewal is unfolding perfectly, even if the progress isn't as immediate as we might hope.

It's important to mention here that as we grow in our relationship with God, it can become easy—sometimes without realizing it—to fall into the trap of self-righteousness. This often happens when we begin to experience the beauty of transformation through the Holy Spirit—when God starts to open our eyes to deeper spiritual truths, when we begin to see real changes in our thoughts, behaviors, and choices, and when our lives start reflecting more peace, love, and purpose. In these moments, the enemy tries to twist our progress into pride by planting seeds of judgment, comparison, and superiority. This subtle attack often comes in the form of a religious or legalistic spirit, also known as a modern-day Pharisee spirit. It tempts us to look down on others who may not yet understand what we now see, or who are simply at a different stage of their walk with Christ.

But we must be on guard. **None of us is qualified to judge others; judgment belongs solely to God!** Every revelation we receive, every transformation we undergo, is the work of God's grace in us, not something we earned or achieved on our own. He alone deserves all the glory. If we sense pride, judgment, or spiritual superiority creeping in, we must immediately recognize that it is not from God, but a temptation from the enemy meant to divide and distort.

In those moments—and whenever we sense **any form** of spiritual attack—we must take authority in the name of Jesus.

This declaration is powerful not only against spirits of pride or judgment, but **against any ungodly, impure, tormenting, or oppressive spirit** that tries to interfere with the peace and freedom we have in Christ. As Titus 2:15 teaches us, **"...rebuke with all authority."** So, speak these words out loud with faith and authority:

"In the mighty name of our LORD Jesus Christ, and by the power of His blood, I rebuke every ungodly, impure, and tormenting spirit. I bind your influence, I break every legal right you claim, and I command you to leave me now and never return. I command you to never harm anyone ever again! I seal myself, my home, and my loved ones under the blood of Jesus Christ. Holy Spirit, fill every part of me, my family, and this space with Your holy presence, peace, and power. My family and I belong to our LORD Jesus Christ—and to Him only. Amen."

By declaring this, we humble ourselves before God and stay spiritually protected. We realign our hearts with the truth: that any growth in holiness is by His Spirit, not our strength. We are being renewed daily, not to become proud, but to become more like Christ—walking in love, humility, and grace with every step of faith we take.

As I continued to grow in the Word and allowed the Holy Spirit to do His refining work in me, I began to realize that what I was experiencing wasn't just personal—it was part of something much bigger. My transformation wasn't happening in a vacuum. I was being awakened into a greater move of God that is unfolding all around the world even today. That's when I came across a passage in Acts 2:17–21 (NIV) that spoke directly to everything I had been encountering through the Holy Spirit. It felt as though those words had been written specifically for my journey—confirming that the supernatural experiences I was having were not isolated events, but part of a global outpouring of God's Spirit. The Scripture reads:

"In the last days, God says, I will pour out My Spirit on all people. Your sons and daughters will prophesy, your young men will see visions, your old men will dream dreams. Even on my servants, both men and women, I will pour out My Spirit in those days, and they will prophesy. I will show wonders in the heavens above and signs on the earth below, blood and fire and billows of smoke. The sun will be turned to darkness and the moon to blood before the coming of the great and glorious day of the LORD. And everyone who calls on the name of the LORD will be saved."

This powerful passage—originally spoken by the prophet Joel—describes the very days we're living in now: a time marked by the outpouring of the Holy Spirit, prophetic revelations, visions, and dramatic signs that call us to repentance and salvation through Jesus Christ.

As I read those verses, it struck me again: the Bible isn't just a record of the past—it's a living, breathing message unfolding in real time. The promises in Scripture no longer felt abstract—they became living realities that I was walking into. The same Spirit Who inspired those words is still moving today, pouring out truth, power, and revelation to those willing to receive. My story—and yours—is part of this divine narrative still being written by the hand of God. And I know, with all my heart, that what He is doing in me, He desires to do in all of us. This is our moment to respond—to step into the greater move of God that is already underway.

Let's pause here for a moment: God shows us wonders in the skies and on Earth, and these signs aren't just random events—they are part of a bigger plan unfolding right in front of us. They're not coincidences, but intentional messages from our Divine Creator, urging us to pay close attention. These signs invite us to see the spiritual truths in our world and to be a part of His greater narrative. By noticing and understanding these wonders, we are being asked to respond and to align ourselves with God's love and purpose.

Today, many people are noticing a rise in spiritual activity and miraculous events that can't be easily explained. From extraordinary healings to unexpected prophetic visions and audible divine revelations, these occurrences are becoming more abundant. More and more individuals are awakening to the undeniable reality of God's existence. As we observe the skies and our surroundings, we are encountering signs that invite us to pay attention to the spiritual truths being revealed. Can we afford to ignore these Divine messages and the testimonies of Jesus any longer? It's time to awaken to the reality of God's presence among us and respond to His invitation to deepen our faith.

We are being invited to open our hearts and minds to the reality of God's presence in our lives. The miracles and signs we witness are not random; they are invitations to grow closer to Him, to see the spiritual truths unfolding before us, and to recognize the urgency of the time in which we live. Just as the Bible foretold, these signs are here to guide us, urging us to respond to God's call and seek His truth more earnestly than ever before. Let us not overlook these divine messages. They serve as powerful reminders that the Bible is not just ancient history—it is alive, relevant, and filled with prophecies that are coming to fruition right before our eyes.

This revelation tied everything together: the resistance to reading the Word, the transformation of my heart, the authority we have in Christ, and now, the confirmation that we are living in prophetic times. These signs are not random—they are divine invitations to pay attention, to draw near, and to live fully awakened to God's presence. The same Spirit that breathed life into the Scriptures is breathing life into us today. Let us not ignore it. Let us respond, with open hearts, ready to be part of God's unfolding story.

Chapter 7

Reconciliation with Our Creator

Experiencing Jesus' pure love, tender compassion, and mercy has shown me that He simply desires to be our friend. **This isn't about religion; it's about developing a personal relationship by getting to know Him and what He is all about**. Jesus calls us to be His followers, **not** to follow any man-made denominations or religions. He wants us to come to Him, to confide in Him during times of sadness, grief, or even contentment, because He loves us deeply. His love is unconditional! God loves us so much that we cannot possibly fathom the depth of His love. In our physical state, we are unable to fully accept or feel the intensity of His love. We only experience a small portion of it now. If you were in the presence of His full love for just one second, the intensity would be so overwhelming that every cell in your body would explode into countless atoms, and each one of those atoms would be praising God. If only we could feel that, even for a split second.

And yet, despite His immense love for us, we often fail to recognize Him in our daily lives. He asks us to acknowledge Him daily, simply by thinking of Him and giving thanks in all circumstances. When life becomes overwhelming, He wants us to turn to Him for help. Our busy lives can sometimes push Him to the background, relegating Him to an afterthought—this is something that breaks His heart.

It's easy to think that as long as we're doing good works—helping others, living by moral standards, and striving to make the world a better place—we're guaranteed a place in heaven. Why, then, are those who do good works—those who may never have considered themselves followers of Christ—**not accepted** by God? The reason is that they don't **acknowledge** Him. They may live selflessly, doing good for others, but without recognizing the One who gave them the ability to do so, they miss the most important relationship of all. The One who breathes life into their lungs each day, who desires to be known, is the source of everything they do— and the key to everything they seek.

It was only after I was saved that I truly began to grasp the extent of God's longing for us to acknowledge not only His creation but, above all, **His existence**. Consider a loving parent whose children, caught up in their busy lives, forget to call or even send a simple message. The parent reaches out repeatedly, yet the children are too preoccupied, remembering their parent only when they need something. After years of this, imagine the parent's heartache. Though forgotten, the parent continues to love and wait patiently, longing for their children to reach out.

This is how God feels about His children who fail to acknowledge His existence amidst life's demands. God desires closeness with you. He longs for His children to return to Him. He misses you immensely, though you may not realize it. He waits patiently for us to come to Him willingly. No matter what the child does, the parent's love remains constant, seeing past the mistakes. This is how God views you – with eyes of pure love and boundless compassion.

Here's another metaphor: it's like a relationship between a husband and a wife. Imagine they get married, and then— boom—the wife stops talking to her husband… for months.

She doesn't call, doesn't text, doesn't even leave a sticky note on the fridge. That kind of relationship? Yeah, it's not going to thrive. At best, it's cold. At worst, it's over. And that's exactly what God *doesn't* want with us. He's not looking for a wedding day commitment followed by months of silence. He's longing for daily connection—a living, breathing relationship where we talk to Him, not just when we need a miracle or can't find our car keys. He wants real conversation, real trust, and real love—because He's a real God Who's madly in love with you.

My dear friends, let's acknowledge God more frequently throughout the day by praising and thanking Him for everything, regardless of our situations. Remember: the more our praises and thanksgivings rise, the more His blessings and rewards flow down.

We often underestimate God's unconditional love for us and His willingness to endure our shortcomings. We must choose to seek Him first—this is where our **free will** comes into play. He patiently waits for us to come to Him, respecting and honoring our free will. We must choose Him first, for He will never force us to love Him. Just as every meaningful human relationship requires mutual affection, true love can only exist with free will. Our faithful Heavenly Father patiently waits for us to return to Him, seeing us as lost sheep who have gone astray. Christ loves you with the tender care of a shepherd who loves His sheep.

This truth is confirmed by the Bible, in the book of Matthew 18:12-14 (NIV): **"What do you think? If a man owns a hundred sheep, and one of them wanders away, will he not leave the ninety-nine on the hills and go to look for the one that wandered off? And if he finds it, truly I tell you, he is happier about that one sheep than**

about the ninety-nine that did not wander off. In the same way Your Father in heaven is not willing that any of these little ones should perish."

These verses express God's incredible joy over each person He brings back to Himself! Jesus tells this story to show how deeply God cares for every individual, even if they stray away. He will go after the lost, leaving the ninety-nine in safety, just to find the one that's wandered.

God doesn't just love the group as a whole — He loves you personally! If you ever feel distant, lost, or unsure, this passage is saying that you matter so much to God that He would come looking for you, never giving up until He finds you. And when He does? There's great celebration in heaven — because God delights in bringing you back into His embrace! He doesn't want anyone to be left behind.

Even if we stray or feel disconnected from our faith, God doesn't wait passively for us to return. **He pursues us, often through circumstances, people, or spiritual encounters, calling us back into a relationship with Him.** This concept of God's relentless pursuit of the lost provides comfort and hope, reassuring us that no matter how far we wander, we are never too far from His reach.

It's exciting to think about: even if you feel like just one small sheep in a vast world, you are incredibly valued and sought after by a God who cares deeply for you as an individual. God's greatest desire is for you to willingly choose Him and be united with Him through Jesus Christ forever!

To deepen your understanding of Jesus as our Shepherd, I encourage you to watch the documentary **Jesus, The Soul Shepherd**, on the Expedition Bible YouTube channel—after you've finished reading my book, of course! It offers valuable insight into His role as our Shepherd.

Chapter 8

Get to Know Our Heavenly Father Personally

Faith runs deep. A superficial understanding of someone does not equate to truly knowing them, let alone trusting them. Why are celebrities so popular? Because, deep down, everyone creates their own image of who they think that person is. Many do the same with God's Son, Jesus Christ. They don't take the time to know God or His Son personally; instead, they settle for others' interpretations of who Jesus is. Try to avoid forming your conclusions about Jesus just based on what others have shared with you. Take the time to explore and understand for yourself.

How many false portrayals of Jesus exist today? Millions. Every Sunday, you hear a pastor's interpretation of who they think Jesus Christ is. In many organized churches, there's a distorted perception of who Jesus truly is. This isn't genuine faith; how can you truly have faith or trust in someone you don't really know? This misrepresentation of Jesus by **self-appointed** ministers and pastors is one of the biggest challenges we face today.

We wouldn't form opinions about our friends based on what others say without ever speaking to them ourselves. Yet, many do exactly that with Jesus. I made the same mistake—learning about Him from others instead of seeking to know Him personally. Jesus warns us against this. We do not learn about our Heavenly Father through other men; we learn about our Heavenly Father from Father Himself!

My dear friends, I encourage you to get to know Jesus Christ personally. That's how your faith and trust in Him will grow. True faith flourishes when you have His Son in your heart and truly know Him. Ultimately, you will carry this light in your heart, soul, and spirit, cultivating a genuine love for our Divine Creator.

Take the time to know your true Heavenly Father through prayer. Ask Him to reveal the truth. In Ephesians 1:17-21, the Apostle Paul expresses a heartfelt prayer asking God to grant believers wisdom and revelation so that they may know God more intimately. He also highlights the hope of our calling and the richness of our inheritance:

"I keep asking that the God of our LORD Jesus Christ, the Glorious Father, may give you the Spirit of wisdom and revelation, so that you may know Him better. I pray that the eyes of your heart may be enlightened in order that you may know the hope to which He has called you, the riches of His glorious inheritance in His holy people, and His incomparably great power for us who believe. That power is the same as the mighty strength He exerted when He raised Christ from the dead and seated Him at His right hand in the heavenly realms, far above all rule and authority, power and dominion, and every name that is invoked, not only in the present age but also in the one to come." (Ephesians 1:17-21, NIV).

You can also pray for our glorious God to reveal Himself to you and to help you know Him better, both for yourself and for your friends and family.

Here is another Bible verse that emphasizes God's desire for people to know Him and to grow in their knowledge of their Heavenly Father:

"Thus says the LORD:

'Let not the wise man glory in his wisdom,

Let not the mighty man glory in his might,

Nor let the rich man glory in his riches;

But let him who glories glory in this,

That he understands and knows Me,

That I AM the LORD, exercising lovingkindness, judgment, and righteousness in the earth.

For in these I delight,' says the LORD." (Jeremiah 9:23-24, NKJV).

These verses encourage people to take pride **not** in worldly achievements but in their understanding and knowledge of our everlasting Father.

A true understanding of our Creator, our Heavenly Father, leads to authentic faith and genuine love in your heart for Him, His Son, and ultimately for others. Soon, true faith will shine through all who are truly His children, revealing the hearts of many. All that's left to do is call on His Son daily, accept Him into your heart, and allow God to work His miracles both within you and around you. Turn to your God. Seek His face. Give Him your heart, and trust Him to do the rest.

Chapter 9

Global Unrest. "TIME IS SHORT"

In 2023, one unforgettable moment stands out vividly in my mind. I was deeply immersed in prayer, fervently seeking to understand God's Will for my life and the path He desires for me. As I meditated on this profound question, the very atmosphere around me seemed to pulse with divine energy. Then, in an instant, a voice cut through the silence of my home. The words that pierced through were simple yet immensely powerful: "Time is short." I was home all alone, and the weight of those words settled over me with a sense of urgency and purpose that I can't fully describe. It was as if the Divine was calling me to action, urging me to embrace the precious time I have and to live with a renewed sense of mission.

In the days that followed, I learned that other believers had received the same message. This wasn't just a personal encounter—it was a shared experience, divinely orchestrated. When people who have never met receive the same prompting from God, it points to something larger—a message for the faith community, not just the individual. It confirmed what many of us are already sensing—God is stirring His people, calling us into alignment, unity, and readiness.

This unity of experience among believers is a reflection of what the Bible teaches in 1 Corinthians 12:12-27: just as a physical body has many parts, each with its unique role, the Body of Christ is made up of diverse members, each vital to

God's mission. Saved believers, through their connection to Jesus, work together like different parts of a single body—each one playing a distinct, yet essential, role. Jesus Christ is the Head of this Body, guiding and empowering every believer **through the Holy Spirit**, Who unites and strengthens us. This spiritual connection means that we are not isolated; we are part of a larger community, working together to spread truth, love, and goodness in the world. Later in this book, you will learn about the supernatural gifts that come from the Holy Spirit when believers are saved and filled with His presence—gifts that empower us to fulfill God's will on earth.

One of the most remarkable signs of this unity is the way saved believers often receive similar divine messages or revelations around the same time. This shared experience serves as a powerful testament to the authenticity of our faith and the work of the Holy Spirit within us. It reinforces the idea that we are all tuned into the same source—Jesus Christ. As a result, we can easily recognize others who are truly saved, not just by words, but by their strong connection to Christ. Their lives visibly reflect a genuine relationship with Him and a deep commitment to living according to His teachings, all empowered by the Holy Spirit.

As I continued to reflect on the message, "Time is short," I couldn't help but notice how the world itself seemed to echo those words. News headlines, conversations, and even casual observations began to take on new weight. Suddenly, what once felt like distant chaos became a personal wake-up call. The growing global unrest and volatility we are witnessing serve as a stark reminder of the fragile nature of our world today. We can no longer ignore the signs around us. This deepening instability creates an urgent need to reflect on the message many believers, myself included, have received: "Time is short." This divine communication is not merely a warning; it is a call to action, encouraging us that we must prioritize our relationship with God now more than ever. Tomorrow is not promised, and the time to respond to God's call is now. Our lives are fleeting—gone in the blink of an eye.

The enemy knows this truth all too well. Satan is ramping up his attacks, sowing division, confusion, and fear both globally and on a personal level, because he knows his time is running out. His influence is intensifying, seeking to distract, deceive, and derail as many as possible. This growing darkness should not cause us to fear but to urgently turn to the marvelous light of Christ. In a world where expressions of faith are often met with skepticism or even scorn, the urgency of "Time is short" becomes even clearer. It serves as a divine nudge to realign our hearts, placing God above all else, especially as the enemy works overtime in these last days. With global conflicts, societal changes, and pandemics on the rise, the need to invite Christ into our hearts through prayer has never been more crucial. This is the moment to surrender control, allowing God to take the wheel of your life and guide you through these turbulent times.

"The point of prophesy is for God to prove that He is God. There is comfort in knowing exactly what is happening as you see it unfolding. You don't have to be afraid because you know what is going to happen next." Additionally, *"It's a wonderful thing to realize that God didn't give us Bible prophecy to scare us, He gave us Bible prophecy to prepare us. We get to know what's happening next and we have great hope."* These lines are from the **2017** documentary **The Coming Convergence**,

which explores biblical prophecies and how they are unfolding in our modern world.

It highlights geopolitical events, natural disasters, and societal shifts as signs that prophecy is no longer just something we read about—it's something we're living through. Watching these ancient predictions come alive in real-time left me both awestruck and grounded. These fulfillments reminded me that the God Who authored the beginning has also written the end—and everything in between. That realization brought me a kind of peace that only comes when you know you're held by the One Who already knows how the story finishes.

Since that film's release, we've witnessed even more significant developments—nations aligning against Israel, intensifying global conflicts, waves of natural disasters, pestilence, and the rise of advanced technology creeping into nearly every part of life. These aren't just headlines; they're like flashing neon signs pointing straight back to Scripture. Suddenly, prophecy doesn't feel so distant. It feels present. It feels personal.

But here's the beautiful part: this isn't meant to scare us. It's meant to open our eyes, give us clarity, and stir up a little holy hope. My beloved, this is our invitation to live expectantly—not with panic, but with purpose. Seeing these ancient prophecies unfold in real time didn't make me hide under a blanket with canned goods and a flashlight (although, I won't lie, the thought crossed my mind once or twice). What it really did was ground me. It reminded me that the God Who began the story in Genesis is **the same One** Who brings it to completion in Revelation—and He hasn't lost control for a second. And knowing that? It brings a kind of peace that no headline or breaking alert could ever steal.

In light of these prophetic fulfillments, we also need to recognize the responsibility that comes with them. Jesus Himself urges us to speak up—not just the preachers or the authors or the people with microphones. All of us. In Matthew 10:27, He says, **"What I tell you in the dark, speak in the daylight; what is whispered in your ear, proclaim from the rooftops."** If He's placed something on your heart—whether it's through prayer, Scripture, or even a quiet nudge—you weren't meant to keep it to yourself.

So yes, that means even if you're 'that person' who brings Jesus into a casual conversation, or who mentions repentance at a dinner table, it's worth it. Awkward or not, people need to hear what God has done in our lives. They need to hear our testimonies. The Gospel isn't something to keep hidden; it's the greatest news the world could ever receive—life-giving, soul-rescuing, heaven-celebrating news! And if that makes us seem a bit "out there," then we're in good company. They thought Jesus was out there too—and they crucified the **only perfect, holy Man** Who ever lived. But His message didn't die with Him, and neither should ours.

Now, let's talk about that popular phrase: "Faith is a personal matter." It sounds polite. Respectful, even. But if you look closer, it's one of the enemy's favorite lies. Why? Because it keeps us quiet. It makes us hesitant. And it convinces us that silence is safer than obedience. Satan knows that the power of the Gospel—the Good News—lies not just in believing it quietly, but in boldly sharing it with others. If he can convince us that our faith should be kept private, he effectively stifles our witness and weakens our impact. This mindset breeds fear, hesitation, and spiritual passivity. But Jesus never told us to keep our faith quiet—He told us to go into all the world and proclaim it (Mark 16:15).

The enemy wants us tame. He wants us passive. But the truth? Your story, your testimony, your voice—it carries the power to awaken someone else's heart. To stir hope. To break chains. And perhaps even to save someone's life. Faith was never meant to be locked away in our journals or whispered behind closed doors. It's meant to be lived out loud, shared boldly, and drenched in love.

God's heart is so clear: He wants **"all people to be saved and to come to a knowledge of the truth"** (1 Timothy 2:4, NIV). And guess what? You get to be part of that rescue mission. Not by force. Not by pressure. But by love—real, Spirit-filled, courageous love. Because someone out there needs to hear what you've got to say. Someone needs your voice. And time, dear friend… is short.

And that urgency becomes deeply personal when we consider the people we love—especially those who are suffering or facing the end of their lives. Whether they're battling illness, walking through grief, or caught in the chaos of war, one thing remains true: they need hope, and they need it now. The kind of hope that doesn't expire. The kind that only Jesus can offer.

Everyone deserves to know that **only Christ alone can save a soul**. We never know when our last opportunity to speak up will come—and delaying may mean missing that chance forever. And let's be honest: if Jesus is the only One Who can rescue your loved ones from eternal separation from God, **why on earth would you keep Him to**

yourself? This isn't about being preachy—it's about being loving. Really loving.

God's heart is that none should perish but that **all** would come to repentance (2 Peter 3:9). And guess how He reaches them? Through us. Through our courage, our compassion, and our conversations. You don't have to have all the answers. You just have to be willing to speak up.

And guess what? One day, when you stand before our Father in Heaven and He asks, "Why didn't you accept Jesus as your LORD and Savior?"—there will be no excuse. Because He will show **your life review**, and in it, you'll see every moment He reached out to you. Every messenger He sent. Every divine appointment. Every conversation like this one. And how, again and again, you still turned away. That moment won't be about shame—it will be about truth. A truth that was offered in love but refused in pride.

So if you're reading this now, know this: this is one of those moments. This is one of those messengers. And I'm here to plead with you—don't reject the truth.

That said, our job isn't to pressure or persuade anyone into faith. We're not spiritual salespeople. We're messengers of a gracious God. He never forces Himself on anyone, and neither should we. He invites, and we echo that invitation—with gentleness, humility, and love.

So we speak—not because we're trying to win an argument, but because we care deeply. And even that care isn't from us—it's stirred by the Holy Spirit within us. We plant seeds and water them with prayer, trusting Him to do what only He can do. When we share truth with love and patience, we honor both the dignity of others and the sacred gift of free will that God has given to each person.

Let your faith shine, not shove. Point others to Jesus with sincerity, not superiority or judgment. After all, we're not the heroes of the story—Jesus is.

Now, let's briefly talk about the other side of the coin— what happens when someone hears the truth and still chooses to walk away.

Without accepting Christ's sacrifice on the cross, a person **remains without the forgiveness of sins,** which is absolutely necessary for eternal life with God. John 3:36 (NIV) lays it out clearly: **"Whoever believes in the Son has eternal life, but whoever rejects the Son will not see life, for God's wrath remains on them."** This is not just a philosophical idea or a theological debate—it's real. It's the reality of our lives and the eternal fate of our souls.

But hear me clearly: God doesn't want that outcome for anyone. 1 Thessalonians 5:9 (NKJV) assures us, **"For God did not appoint us to wrath, but to obtain salvation through our LORD Jesus Christ."** His heart has always been to rescue, not condemn. That's why the cross wasn't a symbol—it was a rescue mission. Jesus took the wrath we deserved so we could walk in a freedom we could never earn.

This is the depth of His love: while we were still sinners, Christ died for us (Romans 5:8). Not when we had it all together. Not when we proved ourselves worthy. But when we were a mess. That's Grace.

So what do we do with this truth? We lift our eyes. Colossians 3:2 (NIV) says, **"Set your minds on things**

above, not on earthly things." We stop getting distracted by the temporary, and we start living for what's eternal.

Jesus taught us not to hoard treasures here on earth, where they decay, disappoint, and can be taken, but to store up treasures in heaven—souls reached, love given, truth spoken (See Matthew 6:19–21).

And here's the really beautiful part—God doesn't just call us to labor for His Kingdom and then forget our efforts. Nope! God sees it all. Every step of obedience. Every moment you choose courage over comfort. Every tear you've cried in prayer. And even that awkward time when you opened your mouth to talk about Jesus and they looked at you like you had five heads. None of it is wasted. Not a single thing. He's keeping track in ways that would put the best spreadsheets to shame.

Hebrews 6:10 (NIV) promises us, **"God is not unjust; He will not forget your work and the love you have shown Him as you have helped His people and continue to help them."** That means He keeps track—like, eternal-record-keeping kind of track. And unlike your earthly job, where you might get a mug and a handshake at retirement, the rewards He's planning? Out of this world—literally.

Jesus Himself said in Matthew 10:42 (NIV), **"If anyone gives even a cup of cold water to one of these little ones who is my disciple, truly I tell you, that person will certainly not lose their reward."** Did you catch that? A cup of water. That's barely effort. That's like tossing someone a bottle of water—they don't even break a sweat, and God still counts it. Because to Him, it's not about the size of the gesture—it's about the love behind it. He sees it, He values it, and He never forgets.

One day, when we stand before Him, we'll see the ripple effect of our obedience—things we didn't even realize mattered. That time you encouraged someone? Planted a seed. That moment you said, "God loves you"? Watered it. And maybe someone else saw it grow. But in the end, we all rejoice together. As 1 Corinthians 3:8-9 (NIV) says, **"The one who plants and the one who waters have one purpose, and they will each be rewarded according to their own labor. For we are co-workers in God's service…"**

And best of all, Revelation 22:12 (NIV) gives us this beautiful promise straight from Jesus' own mouth: **"Look, I AM coming soon! My reward is with Me, and I will give to each person according to what they have done."** Now let's be clear—**Jesus is the greatest reward of all.** To see Him face to face, to dwell in His presence forever, and to finally be made like Him—that's the ultimate prize. But in His goodness, He also promises other rewards—crowns of righteousness, joy, and life; eternal glory, immortal bodies that will never decay; and the unfading inheritance prepared for those who love Him (1 Corinthians 15:52–53).

He's not just bringing heaven with Him—He's bringing recognition, celebration, and joy for every act of obedience you offered in love. Can you imagine that moment? The King above all kings looking you in the eye and saying, **"Well done, good and faithful servant!"** (Matthew 25:21, NIV). That moment beats any trophy, paycheck, or glowing five-star review here on earth!

Now, I know what you might be thinking: *"That all sounds great—but what if people don't understand me? What if they ridicule or reject me?"* And that brings us to something crucial. We're not here to win popularity contests—we're here to please God. Yes, even when it's uncomfortable. Even when it's awkward. Even when it means risking that blank stare or awkward silence when we bring up Jesus. Because, friend, let's be real: the fear of rejection is nothing compared to the joy of obedience—and the eternity that might be changed because of it.

As Paul boldly put it in Galatians 1:10 (NIV): **"Am I now trying to win the approval of human beings, or of God? Or am I trying to please people? If I were still trying to please people, I would not be a servant of Christ."** That verse is a mirror. It helps us check our hearts. Who are we living for—God or the crowd? Are we living to please people, or are we living to please God?

When we live to please God, we not only walk in His will, but we also receive boldness to speak truth in love. And let's be honest—the Gospel isn't always easy to share. It's **countercultural.** It calls for repentance. It points to the only way to salvation through Jesus Christ. But it is the most powerful, life-changing message in the universe. And you, dear friend, get to be a messenger of it.

Being on God's team is the highest honor and the greatest achievement of all. It's not just meaningful—it's **eternally significant.** Sure, people might roll their eyes, unfriend you, or call you crazy—but hey, **let them talk.** Because the glory that awaits you far outweighs any awkward moment you face now (see Romans 8:18). Keep your eyes on eternity. Keep your heart open to every soul God places in your path.

If you're hesitant—afraid of saying the wrong thing or being ridiculed—remember this: you're not here for applause. You're here for obedience. You're here for truth. You're here for souls.

And finally—let me ask you something that might sting a little, but it's asked in love: Would you really let someone you care about slip into eternity without God, just because you were more concerned with their opinion than their salvation? Are you going to let fear, hesitation, or social pressure keep you from sharing the one message that could change their forever?

Don't let that be your story. **Stand strong. Speak the truth. Love boldly. Eternity is waiting.**

Chapter 10

Exposing Deceptions

There's a belief that's become popular today—many people, including some religious leaders and public figures, say, "Every religion leads to the same God, same salvation." Religions that do not proclaim the exclusivity of salvation through Jesus Christ alone, directly contradict the clear message of Scripture. This teaching is a devastating deception, directly opposing the Bible's clear message that salvation comes only through Jesus Christ. Jesus Himself said, **"I AM the way, the truth, and the life. No one comes to the Father except through Me. If you had known Me, you would have known My Father also; and from now on you know Him and have seen Him."** (John 14:6-7, NKJV). And in 1 Timothy 2:5 (NLT), it says, **"For there is one God and one Mediator Who can reconcile God and humanity—the Man Christ Jesus."**

These and other verses throughout the Scripture emphasize the exclusivity of Christ as the sole mediator between God and humanity, affirming that salvation is only through Him. 1 John 5:20 further supports this, stating, **"We know also that the Son of God has come and has given us understanding, so that we may know Him Who is true—and we are in Him Who is true—by being in His Son Jesus Christ. He is the true God and eternal life."**

This passage unveils a crucial and irrefutable truth: Jesus is not merely a path to God—**He is God incarnate**! His divine nature underscores the absolute necessity of salvation through Him alone. As 2 Corinthians 4:4-6 (ESV) further reveals: **"In their case the god of this world (satan) has blinded the minds of the unbelievers, to keep them from seeing the light of the gospel of the glory of Christ, Who is the Image of God. For what we proclaim is not ourselves, but Jesus Christ as LORD, with ourselves as your servants for Jesus' sake. For God, Who said, "Let light shine out of darkness," has shone in our hearts to give the light of the knowledge of the glory of God in the face of Jesus Christ."**

The last verse, **"For God, Who said, 'Let light shine out of darkness,' has shone in our hearts to give the light of the knowledge of the glory of God in the face of Jesus Christ,"** establishes a direct connection between Jesus Christ and the glory of God. It shows how the light of God's glory is revealed in the face of Jesus Christ, making Him the visible manifestation of that glory. Jesus is not only a bearer of God's glory, but He is the visible manifestation of it. When we see Jesus, we are seeing the glory of God in human form. This points to the truth that, in His humanity, Jesus is also fully divine, perfectly displaying the character and nature of God. He is the visible, tangible expression of God in the flesh, revealing the fullness of God's glory to humanity. Religions that do not proclaim this exclusivity of salvation through Jesus Christ alone directly contradict the clear message of Scripture. Jesus, as God incarnate, is the only way to salvation, and no other path can lead to true reconciliation with God.

Jesus Christ is called **"the image of God,"** meaning that He is the visible and exact representation of God Himself. This further points to the doctrine of the **Incarnation**—the belief that God became flesh in the person of Jesus Christ.

101

This phrase echoes Colossians 1:15-17 (NKJV), which says, **"Christ is the image of the invisible God, the firstborn over all creation. For *by* Him all things were created that are in heaven and that are on earth, visible and invisible, whether thrones or dominions or principalities or powers. All things were created *through* Him and *for* Him. And He is *before* all things, and *in* Him all things consist."** As the image of God, Jesus not only reveals God to humanity, but does so in a tangible and comprehensible way, making Him not merely a prophet or a teacher, but God in human form. Furthermore, Colossians 2:9 (NLT) affirms, **"For in Christ lives all the fullness of God in a human body."** This underscores the profound mystery of the Incarnation—that in Jesus, the fullness of God dwells in perfect unity with humanity. Through His life, death, and resurrection, Jesus makes the invisible God known in the most personal and intimate way possible. This truth is central to the faith of Christ's followers, as it affirms that Jesus is both fully God and fully man, bridging the gap between humanity and the divine.

Given the profound truth of Jesus as the image of God and the exclusive way He reveals God to humanity, the Bible makes it crystal clear: there is no other way to God except through Christ and His perfect sacrifice for our sins. Acts 4:11-12 (NIV) further confirms this, stating, **"Jesus is the stone you builders rejected, which has become the cornerstone. Salvation is found in no one else, for there is no other name under heaven given to mankind by which we must be saved."** These statements leave no room for ambiguity—salvation is found only in Jesus Christ. To suggest that all religions lead to the same God or the same salvation is a direct contradiction of this biblical truth. Jesus is the exclusive and essential way to salvation, as He is the only one who bridges the gap between humanity and God through His sacrifice.

The Bible actually warns against this kind of universalism—where all religions are blended—especially as we get closer to the end times. Take 2 Timothy 4:3-4, for instance; it talks about how, in the last days, people will tune away from sound doctrine: **"For the time will come when people will not put up with sound doctrine. Instead, to suit their own desires, they will gather around them a great number of teachers to say what their itching ears want to hear. They will turn their ears away from the truth and turn aside to myths."** And that's exactly what's happening today. Many are turning away from the truth of the gospel and embracing myths or teachings that allow them to believe in multiple paths to God.

Jesus also foretold that in the last days, even true believers would be deceived. In Matthew 24:24, He said, **"For false messiahs and false prophets will appear and perform great signs and wonders to deceive, if possible, even the elect."** This prophecy about the great apostasy, or the great falling away from the faith, is further described in 2 Thessalonians 2:3. It speaks of a time when many will abandon the truth and follow deceptive teachings. This will include especially those who have only practiced religion without ever truly knowing Christ on a personal level. We are already seeing this happen today, as people embrace the dangerous lie that all religions are equally valid. The growing acceptance of religious pluralism is a clear sign of the deception that has been spreading these last days. Sadly, this deception is leading many astray—perhaps even those who once stood firm in the faith—through false teachings and signs that seem convincing but are ultimately lies.

We must remain vigilant and seek God daily to reveal and confirm what is true to us, ensuring that we do not fall away from the real truth. 1 Timothy 4:1 warns that some will abandon their faith and follow **"deceiving spirits and things taught by demons."** The spread of this deception is a clear sign of the times we live in, but we are called to stand firm in the truth of the gospel. Galatians 1:8 reveals to us, **"But even if we or an angel from heaven should preach a Gospel other than the one we preached to you, let them be under God's curse!"** It's a strong warning against anyone who would pervert the gospel or introduce false ideas about salvation—whether by claiming that other religions can lead to God, or suggesting that salvation is found through any means other than repentance and faith in Christ alone.

As true believers, we must reject the lies of pluralism and cling to the truth of Christ. Jesus is the only way to salvation, and we must boldly proclaim this truth in a world that desperately needs it.

Another dangerous deception already present revolves around the idea of aliens, and it will only become more pronounced in the years to come. While many people may dismiss the idea of extraterrestrial beings, the concept is being woven into modern culture, media, and even scientific discourse. Movies, TV shows, books, and news reports about UFO sightings are flooding our screens, slowly desensitizing society to the notion of otherworldly visitors. However, this idea will soon take a darker turn. As the world nears the fulfillment of end-times prophecies, the reality of millions of people being raptured in the twinkle of an eye—what followers of Christ call the Rapture—will be met with an explanation rooted in this growing alien abduction narrative. The media and influential voices will push the idea that these disappearances are a result of extraterrestrial intervention. It will serve to divert attention from the true spiritual reason for this event—the Rapture of the Body of Christ, to gather His faithful followers before God's wrath is poured out on the earth.

The Rapture will happen suddenly, and the world will be left scrambling for answers. The Rapture is a future event described in the Bible, where Jesus will gather all true believers—those who have repented and trusted in Him—up to Heaven. This event is not His physical return to earth, but a moment when followers of Christ are taken up to meet Him in the air, sparing them from the coming 7-year Tribulation, a time of God's judgment and wrath upon the earth.

1 Thessalonians 4:16-17 (NIV) validates this event: **"For the LORD Himself will come down from heaven, with a loud command, with the voice of the archangel and with the trumpet call of God, and the dead in Christ will rise first. After that, we who are still alive and are left will be caught up together with them in the clouds to meet the LORD in the air. And so we will be with the LORD forever."**

Similarly, 1 Corinthians 15:52 (NIV) describes how this will happen: **"In a flash, in the twinkling of an eye, at the *last trumpet*. For the trumpet will sound, the dead will be raised imperishable, and we will be changed."**

This moment will be sudden and unexpected, and it marks the beginning of a period of 7-year Tribulation on earth. Believers, both living and deceased, will be transformed with new, imperishable, and glorified bodies and taken to be with

Jesus, forever removed from the intense suffering to come. The Rapture is a promise of a blessed hope for followers of Christ, assuring them that they will be united with Him in the air before the earth faces the hardest times to come.

We will escape the wrath of God on this earth, leaving the world in confusion and desperate to explain it away. Instead of recognizing the Rapture, the growing narrative of extraterrestrial involvement will emerge, offering a false explanation that these disappearances are the work of aliens, among other deceptive theories. It will serve to distract from the true reason behind these occurrences. The deception will be powerful, and many will be led astray, embracing lies in a world eager to adopt an alternative explanation for the divine intervention unfolding before their eyes. People will be urged to accept this new reality, their faith in God replaced by worship of false explanations and misleading theories. The timing of this deception will be strategic, emerging during a time of widespread panic and fear, making it even harder for many to recognize the truth.

My beloved, I strongly encourage you to watch the documentary **Before The Wrath** (2020), after you finish reading this book. It explores the biblical narrative of the Rapture, providing a deeper understanding of its implications and its profound significance for believers. The film delves into both the cultural and spiritual aspects of the Rapture, highlighting how this momentous event will not be an accident or random occurrence, but rather the fulfillment of God's divine plan. The subsequent deception that will unfold in the aftermath will be nothing more than a desperate attempt to cover the truth, distracting people from the reality of God's purpose and the blessed hope found in Christ.

People will see this devastating deception as a long-awaited revelation, but for those who are filled with God's Spirit, the truth will become clear. The Bible warns of a time when the world will be flooded with lies, and many will be led astray. However, for believers who remain steadfast, our faithful Heavenly Father promises to give wisdom, discernment, and strength to stand firm in the face of such an overwhelming deception. The call is clear: do not be swayed by the lies of the enemy. Seek salvation today and trust in God's ultimate plan for His people, so that you may also be spared from His wrath upon the earth.

Now that we've uncovered these deceptions, let's move forward and expose more of the enemy's dangerous lies. In today's world, the allure of quick answers and instant solutions is more tempting than ever. Many people, driven by desperation, curiosity, or a desire for guidance, are turning to practices such as psychics, tarot card readings, palm readings, tea or coffee readings, astrology, crystals, energy healing practices, Reiki, and mediums—just to name a few. Even more dangerously, some are exploring mind-altering substances like psychedelic drugs, including DMT, in search of mystical experiences, Kundalini awakenings, or out-of-body experiences.

I was once guilty of dabbling in some of these things too...

But these aren't just modern wellness trends. They're spiritual traps, cleverly repackaged from ancient occult rituals. The New Age movement has masked old deceptions with new language—calling them "enlightenment," "empowerment," or "healing." In truth, they pull people further away from God. Why? Because they shift trust away

from the only true source of life and hope—Jesus Christ—
and redirect it toward mystical experiences, human intuition,
or false spirits.

Our culture has bought into the lie that we can find peace
or answers through "the universe," energy fields, or spiritual
forces apart from God. We've been trained to trust anything
or anyone but Him. But where we place our faith matters
deeply to God.

In Exodus 20:3–5 (NIV), God gives this clear command:
**"You shall have no other gods before Me. You shall not
make for yourself an image in the form of anything in
heaven above or on the earth beneath or in the waters
below. You shall not bow down to them or worship
them; for I, the LORD Your God, AM a jealous God..."**

Anything we elevate above God—even spiritual practices,
people, or ideologies—becomes an idol. Today's idols aren't
golden statues or ancient gods—they're often found in our
pursuit of self-improvement, spiritual highs, or unhealthy
obsession with self or others. When we put our trust in these
things, we turn our hearts away from the living God. Our
heavenly Father calls us to place our faith in Him alone—
because without that faith, it is impossible to please Him.

Scripture is clear that engaging in occult practices is not
harmless—it's disgusting to God and spiritually dangerous to
us. Deuteronomy 18:10–12 (NIV) gives a direct warning:
**"Let no one be found among you who... practices
divination or sorcery, interprets omens, engages in
witchcraft, or casts spells, or who is a medium or
spiritist or who consults the dead. Anyone who does
these things is *detestable* to the LORD."**

These are not outdated rules—they're divine protections. Understand that God is not trying to restrict us; He's warning us about the destructive power behind these practices. When we entertain what God has called detestable, **we step outside of His protection** and give the enemy legal access to wreak havoc in our lives. But God's heart is always to guard us, lead us, and keep us safe in His truth—if we allow Him to lead.

While these practices may appear positive or enlightening, they are not spiritually neutral. They open spiritual doors to deception, bondage, and even demonic possession—bringing devastating consequences! After all, we cannot serve two masters. Jesus made it crystal clear in Matthew 6:24 (NIV): **"No one can serve two masters. Either you will hate the one and love the other, or you will be devoted to the one and despise the other..."** We cannot serve God and also dabble in the enemy's territory. There is **no middle ground** in the spiritual realm—we are either walking in the light of God's truth or drifting into the darkness of the enemy's lies. In the Kingdom of God, there is no gray area. **You are either with Him or against Him.**

The enemy rarely reveals himself openly. Instead, he works subtly, offering what looks like truth, healing, or power—until it's too late. As 2 Corinthians 11:14 (NIV) warns: **"For satan himself masquerades as an angel of light."** This is the essence of spiritual deception. It often begins with something that feels good, looks helpful, or seems insightful. But behind that light is a snare. The psychic's "accuracy," the moment of "clarity" from psychedelics, or the tingling energy in a Reiki session—these may feel spiritual, but they are not from the Holy Spirit. **They are counterfeits.**

One especially deceptive practice today is the awakening of Kundalini energy, common in Eastern spirituality. It teaches that a serpent-like energy lies coiled at the base of the spine, waiting to be awakened. People seek this awakening for spiritual enlightenment, but what they are really encountering is a demonic spirit posing as divine power. Physical manifestations—tremors, ecstatic laughter, altered states, euphoria—may feel like spiritual progress, but the source is not God. In fact, Kundalini's association with the serpent ties directly back to Genesis 3:1, where satan deceived Eve. This is not God's Holy Spirit at work—it is a dangerous counterfeit designed to lead people away from truth.

Scripture repeatedly warns us of this spiritual battle. Ephesians 6:12 (NIV) teaches us: **"For our struggle is not against flesh and blood, but against the rulers, against the authorities, against the powers of this dark world and against the spiritual forces of evil in the heavenly realms."** These deceptive practices are not innocent—they open spiritual doors. People, knowingly or unknowingly, invite oppression, confusion, and sometimes even possession. The enemy's goal is to steal, kill, and destroy (John 10:10). He doesn't mind if it begins with curiosity or personal growth. His only aim is to lead us away from God.

2 Thessalonians 2:9-10 (NIV) issues a sobering warning: **"The coming of the lawless one will be in accordance with how satan works. He will use all sorts of displays of power through signs and wonders that serve the lie, and all the ways that wickedness deceives those who are perishing. They perish because they refused to love the truth and so be saved."**

Whether through false signs, mystical healings, or drug-induced experiences, these deceptions can look convincing—but their true aim is to destroy your life and lead your soul into eternal torment. Proverbs 14:12 (NIV) echoes this truth: **"There is a way that appears to be right, but in the end it leads to death."**

The enemy presents his lies as enlightenment, but in reality, they bring spiritual death. **It takes the focus *away* from God's power and brings it onto human pride, self-reliance, and false sense of control.** We must be vigilant in guarding our hearts, testing every spirit, and staying rooted in God's Word.

Here is a simple and practical way to test or discern the spirits around you: hold everything up to the truth of God's Word. **God's Holy Spirit will always point you to Jesus Christ**—never away from Him—and **will never contradict Scripture or glorify anything other than our LORD Jesus Christ.** The Holy Spirit—and the holy angels sent by our LORD God—will never glorify themselves or draw attention to saints, angels, spiritual guides, or anything that is created by God Himself!

They will never lead you to glorify yourself, claim divinity, or call yourself a god—this is one of the most dangerous lies spreading through today's New Age movement. Likewise, the Holy Spirit will never direct you to worship animals, nature, the moon, the sun, statues, icons, the universe, energy, or mystical forces—only Jesus Christ is to be glorified.

Everything and everyone **must** bow down to Jesus Christ alone.

If any spirit, entity, or presence is willing to receive your worship—or is indifferent to you bowing down before it—it is *not* from God! Every being aligned with the true and living God will always point you to worship Jesus Christ alone.

That's a simple and effective way to test the spirits. **Bow down and begin to worship.** If the spirit accepts your worship instead of **immediately** redirecting it to Jesus, it has revealed its true nature. True angels and servants of God will never accept worship—they will always glorify Christ and point you back to Him.

Why is this so important? Because it directly violates God's command—as clearly stated in Exodus 20:3–5 (NIV), which was mentioned earlier in this chapter: **"You shall have no other gods before Me. You shall not make for yourself an image in the form of anything in heaven above or on the earth beneath or in the waters below. You shall not bow down to them or worship them; for I, the LORD your God, AM a jealous God…"**

Let me emphasize this again: The Holy Spirit and all holy angels **always** glorify our God, Jesus Christ, as the one true LORD and Savior. This truth is echoed throughout the entire Bible. I don't want to overwhelm you with a flood of verses here—but please, don't just take my word for it. Open your Bible. Search it for yourself. Ask God to show you the truth. If you're sincere, He absolutely will.

Here's another instant way to test a spirit: **command it, out loud, in the Name of our LORD Jesus Christ.** Say, **"If you are not from the LORD Jesus Christ, I command** you to flee now and never return in the mighty name of our LORD Jesus Christ."

Dark spirits cannot stand the authority of our LORD Jesus or **admit that Jesus is LORD**—they must flee. The Name of Jesus Christ is above every name—**demons tremble at it, and angels obey it**. There is no higher authority in the spiritual realm, period.

If the presence around you is from God, it will **submit to Jesus Christ and admit that He is our LORD**. If not, it will flee. That's how powerful His Name is.

Why not try it for yourself? You have nothing to lose, and only the truth to gain.

Which brings us to an important question we each need to ask: **Why do we so often place our faith in everything but the power of the Living God?**

Instead of turning to psychics, drugs, astrology, or Eastern mysticism, we are invited to turn to God—our Creator, our Redeemer, our Healer, our Deliverer... our Everything. As Jeremiah 33:3 (ESV) promises: **"Call to Me and I will answer you, and will tell you great and hidden things that you have not known."** God alone holds the truth, the power, and the love we desperately seek. In Him, there is no confusion, no deception, and no bondage—only freedom, peace, and eternal life. So why settle for counterfeit answers when the Living God is calling you to Himself?

Now is the time to recognize these deceptions for what they truly are—tools of the enemy to lead us away from the One true God. Only Jesus can truly heal, and He calls us to place our trust in Him alone. If you are facing challenges,

113

don't turn to counterfeit solutions. Instead, turn to Jesus. He is the way, the truth, and the life, and He promises to heal, restore, and guide us to eternal rest.

The deceptions outlined in this chapter are only a glimpse of the many schemes already at work—and more are coming. Each one is designed to distort the truth of Christ and draw people away from Him. These lies won't always look evil; they may seem logical, compassionate, even wise. But beneath the surface, they are rooted in falsehood and lead to destruction. The tragic reality is that without spiritual discernment and a firm foundation in God's Word, many will fall for them. Only those grounded in truth will recognize the counterfeit. Now more than ever, we must cling to the Word of God, test every spirit, and fix our eyes on Jesus.

Chapter 11

God's Timing and the Battle for Our Souls

There is a rhythm to the universe that only God fully understands. Time itself is one of His creations—crafted not just as a measurement of hours and seasons, but as the divine framework within which His will unfolds. Scripture tells us plainly, **"There is a time to be born and a time to die…"** (Ecclesiastes 3:2). That verse isn't just poetic—it's prophetic. Your life, your breath, your moments on this earth were written by God before you ever took your first step. Every chapter, every season—even the painful ones—are known and seen by Him. You are not an accident. Your timeline is not random. And yet, from the very moment you enter this world, there's a war raging over your soul.

The enemy of our souls—satan—knows that time is not on his side. He is already defeated, already judged, already condemned. But until that final sentence is carried out, he fights with desperate fury. As Jesus warns in John 10:10, **"The thief comes only to steal and kill and destroy."** Why? Because while his fate is sealed, ours is not. The enemy knows that. So he plots. He distracts. He deceives. He knows he can't stop God's timing, but he will do everything in his power to stop you from stepping into it. He will fill your days with anxiety, hopelessness, and noise. He'll twist your worth, distort your desires, and whisper lies into your mind until you question your value, your calling, and even God's love. Satan doesn't need to destroy you in one blow—he only needs to delay your awakening long enough for you to miss what God prepared for you.

Satan fights fiercely because he knows exactly what's at stake: the eternal destiny of our souls. If we never come to know Christ, he has a greater chance to legally claim our souls. He knows that salvation is found in Jesus only, and if we remain separated from God, we are far more susceptible to his influence and lies. Satan's fate is sealed—he has no redemption, no hope, no future. He will never be restored and never again experience God's love. He chose to rebel with full knowledge of the consequences. But we, unlike him, still have hope. That's why he hates us so much. He despises that we have what he forever lost—a future with God. He rages against the fact that God offers us what he can never have again: forgiveness, restoration, and salvation.

As long as we have breath, we have a choice—and as long as we have a choice, we have the chance to choose eternal life in Christ, not destruction with the enemy. And that's exactly what he hates—because every moment you remain alive and undecided is a moment you might turn to Jesus, and once you do, his grip on you is broken forever.

I know this battle intimately—not as a distant concept, but as a personal reality.

Before I came to know Christ, before I was filled with the Holy Spirit, I lived under an invisible war I couldn't fully comprehend. The enemy didn't just come for my circumstances—he came for my mind, my sense of worth, and my hope. He assaulted my thoughts with fear and despair, whispering lies that seemed so real, I began to believe they were my own. He attacked my health, my finances, my relationships—turning my life into a whirlwind of confusion and oppression. But the most dangerous battlefield was my mind. The enemy wanted me to believe that there was no way out, that I was a failure, and that nothing could be better than ending it all. I can still remember the heaviness, the isolation, the sudden, unexplainable thoughts telling me to give up. These thoughts of ending it all came out of nowhere, and they came often. I was completely alone in my suffering—or so I thought. For a time, it worked. I felt overwhelmed and consumed by thick darkness and heaviness, believing that these dark thoughts were my own and that I had no escape.

One evening, just a couple of months **before** I gave my life to Jesus, I was sitting on my bed with my daughter beside me. I blinked for just a moment, and in that brief instant, I saw something that shook me to my core—an ancient, evil entity flying directly at me. It had only half of the body— swift, aggressive, terrifying. In that instant, I knew. This wasn't imagination or fantasy. This was real. The darkness I had been feeling wasn't "just in my head." It was spiritual. I saw how they operate in the unseen realm, sowing fear, confusion, and despair, starting fights out of nowhere, injecting thoughts of suicide like arrows from the shadows. It was terrifying…

And that terrifying moment sparked something unexpected in me: **a question.**

If evil is this real… then good must be real too? If there are demons, then there must be angels. If darkness exists, then surely there is Light.

That moment of terror became the beginning of my search for the truth—for God. It was the turning point that pulled me toward the One true Light. That's when I became desperate to find answers, to seek Him. I share more about that experience in Chapter 3 of this book.

You see, the enemy doesn't just want to make your life difficult—he wants to distract you long enough that you stop seeking truth altogether. He wants you to stop asking questions, to stop searching for answers, to become numb and passive. He knows that time is precious and that you were created for something eternal. His goal is to keep you from discovering who you truly are in Christ—to bury you under layers of unforgiveness, wounds, and confusion so that the truth remains hidden. He wants to destroy you before you ever step into the life God designed for you. And he does it subtly—through pain, fear, disappointment, distractions, and delay.

But once I started questioning everything, the enemy became even more aggressive. It was as if he knew I was getting closer to the truth—and he hated it. Still, through that storm, God was quietly drawing me near. The Light I had once only wondered about began to break through the shadows. The lies I had believed for so long started to unravel beneath the weight of His truth. I came to realize that those destructive thoughts weren't mine—they had been carefully planted by an enemy desperate to destroy me before I ever encountered my Savior. But when I finally surrendered to Christ—when I gave Him my pain, my fear, and my entire heart—everything began to change, and healing finally began.

God's truth cut through the fog. His love cast out the fear. And I began to understand that my life wasn't a lost cause. It was a battlefield—and I had just switched sides. Through the power of the Holy Spirit, I gained discernment to recognize the enemy's tactics and the authority to rebuke these evil forces in Jesus' name. What once had power over me now had no hold. The very mind the enemy tried to enslave became the place where God began to rebuild, restore, and fill with truth.

I came to understand that our Heavenly Father is fighting for us all the time—even when we can't see it. He is the Commander of the armies of heaven, and He defends His children with unmatched power and love. He stands outside of time but enters it for our sake. He sends warnings, messengers, and divine interruptions. He allows hardship not to harm us but to awaken us—to shake us from spiritual slumber and realign our hearts with His will. Because God wants to save your soul out of His great love and mercy, not out of His anger. Sometimes what feels like delay is actually mercy—God's way of giving us space to return, to repent, and to prepare for what He has planned. His timing isn't slow; it's patient. It's never random; it's always purposeful. And more often than not, our darkest nights are not signs of abandonment—they are signs that breakthrough is near. They are the enemy's last desperate attempts to stop what God is about to do.

When your spiritual battle intensifies, it's often because the enemy knows he's about to lose your soul to the light. He sees what you don't yet see: that you are close to freedom. Close to calling. Close to salvation. That's why, in those moments, **do not stop praying. Don't stop crying out to God for help.** You are closer than you think. Keep seeking Him—keep asking, keep knocking. Because **only God** can break those chains. No one else can. I know it because I've lived it.

I've seen the reality of the spiritual realm. I've seen how dark entities move—and I've also seen how they tremble before the presence of God. The same evil spirits that once tormented me now tremble at the name of Jesus. If you only knew how afraid the enemy is of Jesus Christ—and how terrified he is of someone filled with the Holy Spirit—you wouldn't fear him for another second. Once you realize the authority you carry in Christ, once you understand that every demonic force must obey when you speak in **Jesus' name**— you'd laugh at how hard they work just to keep you from discovering it.

That's the enemy's greatest fear: that you'll wake up. That you'll realize who you are in Christ. That you'll stop believing his lies and start using your voice. Because the moment you walk in your God-given authority, **he loses his grip on your life**. These spirits may still try to intimidate, distract, or oppress—but when a believer, filled with the Holy Spirit, speaks with the authority of Jesus, they have **no choice but to flee**.

So don't give up now. Don't back down. Your prayers are shaking the unseen. Your cries are reaching heaven. And your faith—no matter how small it may feel—is enough for God to move. You are not fighting alone. The living God is with you, fighting for you, and ready to fill you with His Spirit. Once He does, everything changes. You will not just survive this battle—you will rise in victory, walking in the authority that was yours all along.

God's timing isn't just about events lining up—it's about **hearts lining up with His**. When your spirit aligns with heaven, things begin to move. Doors open. Burdens lift. Clarity comes. You begin to see not just Who God is, but who you are in Him. And that moment—the moment of surrender and alignment—is one the enemy fears most.

So today, ask yourself: are you aware of the battle for your soul? Have you been drifting, delaying, distracted? Has the enemy been speaking lies to you, trying to distort your worth or break your spirit? If so, remember this: **you don't have to fight alone.** The One Who created time is fighting for you. The cross of Christ already won the war. Now it's up to you to step into that victory, moment by moment, day by day.

You were made for more than this world. Your existence is eternal, and the choices you make now ripple into forever. That's why satan fights so hard—because he's trying to keep you from seeing just how valuable you really are in Christ. But when you step into the light of God's timing, when you surrender your life and say, "Here I am, LORD," everything begins to shift. Bondage breaks. Scales fall off your eyes. And suddenly, what once felt meaningless takes on holy purpose.

The point of this life isn't just to survive. It isn't to gather wealth, build fame, or find fleeting comfort. **The point of this life is to find God, walk with Him daily, and be made whole in Him.** Everything else fades. But what you build with God now is eternal. That's the battle we're in—and that's the victory we can have through Jesus Christ.

Don't let the enemy steal your time. Don't let him delay your destiny any longer. Run to the One Who wrote your story before time began. He's still calling.

And the moment you say yes, everything begins to change.

Chapter 12

Prayer and Worship: Our Ultimate Weapons

The devil relentlessly seeks to destroy us before God's appointed time for us, attacking from every angle—whether through illness, financial hardship, strained relationships, or emotional turmoil. His aim is to undermine our faith and weaken our resolve. He uses diseases, such as cancer and chronic conditions, to drain our strength and fill us with hopelessness. He strikes at our finances, causing instability and anxiety, and he sows discord in our relationships, pitting loved ones against one another. No area of our lives is off-limits to his destructive tactics. He knows that if he can steal our peace and joy, he can cloud our minds with doubt and despair.

In the face of such relentless assaults, prayer becomes our greatest weapon. It fortifies our spirit, aligns us with God's will, and summons divine power to overcome the devil's schemes. Prayer is more than communication with God; it is an act of spiritual warfare that breaks chains, heals wounds, and brings light into darkness. When we pray, we are wielding the spiritual armor that God provides, standing firm against every assault.

The enemy despises our prayer and worship because he knows these are powerful acts that connect us directly to the everlasting presence and power of God. He understands that prayer strengthens our faith, renews our spirit, and draws us closer to God, our ultimate source of hope and victory. By making us feel too tired, busy, or indifferent, he tries to divert our focus from God. He knows that if he can make us **question the effectiveness** of our prayers or the worth of our worship, he weakens our spiritual armor and leads us to drift from God.

This is why prayer and worship are not always easy. Staying committed to daily prayer and consistent worship can feel like a struggle, and often, it's because we are in the midst of a spiritual battle. Have you ever noticed that the moment you begin to pray, something always seems to distract you? A sudden interruption, a racing mind, or a feeling of overwhelming fatigue and sleepiness might pull you away. This happens because the enemy is doing everything in his power to keep us from connecting with God. He wants to disrupt our focus, keep us powerless, and prevent us from experiencing the transformative power of prayer and worship. The battle is real, but it's also a battle we're meant to win, because in every moment of resistance, we are growing stronger in our faith and character. So, when those moments of resistance arise, remember—it's precisely because your prayer and worship are so powerful, and the enemy knows this all too well.

Yet, God's Word provides us with the tools we need to overcome this battle. James 4:7 urges us to **"Submit yourselves therefore to God. Resist the devil, and he will flee from you."** Prayer and worship are our weapons of resistance. When we press through fatigue and distractions, we find renewed strength in God, frustrating the enemy's efforts to undermine our relationship with Him. In moments of prayer and worship, we declare that our hearts and minds belong to God alone. Even when it feels difficult, we reaffirm our commitment to God daily, showing the enemy that we are unshakable in our faith.

The Bible encourages us to pray continually, to keep our connection with God strong and steadfast. Ephesians 6:18 (NIV) teaches us, **"And pray in the Spirit on all occasions with all kinds of prayers and requests. With this in mind, be alert and always keep on praying for all the LORD's people."** This verse highlights the importance of vigilance and steadfastness in prayer, covering ourselves and others in spiritual protection.

Furthermore, 1 Thessalonians 5:16-18 (ESV) simply and powerfully states, **"Rejoice always, pray without ceasing, give thanks in all circumstances; for this is the will of God in Christ Jesus for you."** This passage calls us to maintain a constant spirit of prayer and gratitude, staying connected with God in every aspect of life. Continuous prayer not only strengthens our faith but also equips us to resist the devil's relentless attacks, drawing on the power and protection that only God can provide.

Philippians 4:6-7 (NIV) reinforces this truth, saying, **"Do not be anxious about anything, but in every situation, by prayer and petition, with thanksgiving, present your requests to God. And the peace of God, which transcends all understanding, will guard your hearts and your minds in Christ Jesus."** This scripture teaches us that through prayer, we can release our worries and place them before God, knowing that His peace will guard our hearts and minds.

We are not meant to face this spiritual battle alone, and in our own strength, we are powerless against the enemy's attacks. These evil forces are very ancient and well-versed in how to target our weaknesses. It is essential to understand this crucial truth: we are not meant to rely on our own abilities in this fight. The forces of darkness are far too powerful for us to overcome on our own. Instead, we must lean fully on God's strength to defend us, to protect us, and to defeat the enemy's schemes. By praying continually, we tap into God's unlimited power, which enables us to withstand every attack, overcome every temptation, and resist every attempt by the enemy to pull us away from His truth.

So, how do we remain consistent and persistent in prayer and worship, even when the battle feels overwhelming? The answer is simple—just as I mentioned earlier about reading the Bible, you can do the same here: simply ask God to give you a **deep desire** and **persistence** in prayer and worship, because we were made to worship Him. And that's exactly what He longs for us to do. Don't hesitate to ask God for this—He understands our struggles and sees the spiritual battle we face. God delights in those who make an effort to ask for these things, and He is faithful to grant the desires of a heart that longs to grow closer to Him. This request aligns perfectly, not only with His Word, but more importantly with His will, as He desires us to draw near to Him and rely completely on His strength. After all, we were made to worship Him!

I remember when I first started praying for God to help me cultivate a deeper love for prayer, I noticed a shift. What once felt like a struggle became a joy, and I found myself more eager to spend time with the LORD. So, keep asking, trusting that He will answer, and don't give up until you experience that shift in your heart. Developing these spiritual habits is like building a muscle; it takes time, persistence, and consistent effort. But as long as you ask, God will help you grow in this area, strengthening your resolve and desire to connect with Him.

And as you grow in prayer, it's vital to recognize the incredible authority you've been given in the name of Jesus Christ. The sooner we truly grasp the power that is in His name and His blood, the better equipped we are to stand against the attacks of the enemy. His name is not merely a label—it carries divine power. It is the only name that causes the enemy to tremble and flee, shatters chains, and causes strongholds to crumble. Philippians 2:10-11 declares, **"That at the name of Jesus every knee should bow, in heaven and on earth and under the earth, and every tongue acknowledge that Jesus Christ is LORD, to the glory of God the Father."** When we speak the name of Jesus Christ with faith and authority, we are not using empty words—we are invoking the King above all kings and the LORD above all Lords, whose power has already defeated death, hell, and the grave. The forces of darkness have no choice but to submit to His authority.

Earlier in this book, in Chapter 3, we discussed the LORD's Prayer, where we ask for salvation and the Holy Spirit. At the end of that prayer, we say, **"In the name of the Father, Son, and Holy Spirit."** This is a phrase we often say at the end of the LORD's Prayer when asking for salvation, and it's also commonly used during baptism. Here's why: The phrase "In the name of the Father, Son, and Holy Spirit" acknowledges the fullness of God's nature. God is one, but He exists in three distinct persons: the Father, the Son (Jesus Christ), and the Holy Spirit. When we pray in this way, we are honoring the entire Trinity, affirming that all three persons of God are involved in our salvation and our relationship with Him.

On the other hand, when we pray specifically **"in the name of Jesus Christ,"** we are focusing on the unique authority and power that Jesus, as the Son of God, holds. Jesus is the one who made a way for us to approach God directly. Through His life, death, and resurrection, He bridged the gap between sinful humanity and a holy God. Before Jesus, people couldn't have direct access to God, but because of His sacrifice, we now have the opportunity to have a personal relationship with God. When we pray in Jesus' name, we are acknowledging that it is only through His sacrifice, His power, and His authority that we receive forgiveness, claim victory over life's struggles, intercede for others, and stand against the enemy. His name is the key to unlocking the blessings and power of Heaven, for it is through Jesus that we are reconciled to God and given the chance to receive eternal life.

Right before the darkest battle of my life was about to begin, I had a vivid dream that still resonates with me today. In the dream, I saw dead snakes and scorpions, their lifeless bodies scattered everywhere under my feet. Even though these creatures are often symbols of danger and evil, God was reassuring me in that moment that His power was far greater than any enemy I would face. He was reminding me that nothing would harm me because the snakes and scorpions were already dead under my feet. He already took care of them! God is amazing! Hallelujah!

In that instant, the Holy Spirit brought to my memory the verse from Luke 10:19, where Jesus says, **"I have given you authority to trample on snakes and scorpions and to overcome all the power of the enemy; nothing will harm you."** That verse, along with the imagery in my dream, left me speechless. I was comforted by the powerful truth that the victory over my enemies had already been secured. The power to overcome had already been given to me—and it's available to all of us, whenever we call upon His name with faith. That authority isn't symbolic—it's real, and it changes everything.

Darkness cannot stand in the presence of Jesus. That's why the enemy works so hard to keep people unaware of this truth—because once we grasp it, we become dangerous to the kingdom of darkness. This is why the disciples rejoiced in Luke 10:17, exclaiming, **"LORD, even the demons submit to us in Your name!"** after witnessing the enemy's power crumble before them. The authority given to us through Jesus' name is no small thing. When you feel fear, temptation, tormenting thoughts, or spiritual heaviness—speak the name of Jesus out loud. Say, **"In the name of Jesus Christ, I rebuke these evil spirits. You have no power over me."** You don't need fancy words. The authority is not in how you say it, but in **Whose** name you're saying it.

But that's not all. Jesus makes a bold and empowering promise in John 14:12–14: **"Very truly I tell you, whoever believes in Me will do the works I have been doing, and they will do even greater things than these, because I AM going to the Father. And I will do whatever you ask in My name, so that the Father may be glorified in the Son. You may ask Me for anything in My name, and I will do it."**

These words are astonishing—but they are truth. Jesus isn't just speaking to the apostles; He's speaking to all who believe in Him. He tells us that through faith in Him, we will not only continue His work, but even do greater things because He has gone to the Father and sent us the Holy Spirit. His name is not only a weapon against evil, but also the key to accessing the blessings of Heaven through prayer.

When we pray in His name—with hearts aligned to His will—we are heard, and we are answered. His name carries divine authority, and when we invoke it in faith, Heaven moves on our behalf.

Along with His name, we are also given the powerful covering of **His holy blood**. The blood of Jesus is not a ritual or superstition—it is the very substance of victory that was shed on the cross for our redemption and protection. Revelation 12:11 says, **"They triumphed over him (satan) by the blood of the Lamb and by the word of their testimony."** When Jesus shed His blood on the cross, it became the eternal receipt of victory over sin, death, and the powers of darkness.

The book of Hebrews gives us a powerful explanation of this reality. Hebrews 9:12–15 (NIV) tells us: **"He did not enter by means of the blood of goats and calves; but He entered the Most Holy Place *once for all* by His own blood, thus obtaining *eternal* redemption. The blood of goats and bulls and the ashes of a heifer sprinkled on those who are ceremonially unclean sanctify them so that they are *outwardly* clean. How much more, then, will the blood of Christ, Who through the eternal Spirit offered Himself unblemished to God, cleanse our *consciences* from acts that lead to death, so that we may serve the living God! For this reason Christ is the Mediator of a New Covenant, that those who are called may receive the promised eternal inheritance—now that He has died as a ransom to set them free from the sins committed under the first (old) covenant."**

This passage is essentially saying that, under the old covenant (before Jesus came), people had to offer the blood of animals to symbolically cleanse themselves from sin. But that cleansing was only **outward**—it couldn't reach the heart. It was never meant to be the final solution, but rather a temporary picture of what was to come.

Then Jesus came. (New Testament begins).

He offered His own perfect, sinless blood as a **once-and-for-all sacrifice**. Unlike animal sacrifices, His blood has the power to cleanse our **consciences**, free us from the weight of guilt, and transform us from the inside out. His sacrifice did what no ritual or outward act could ever do—it brought us into direct relationship with God, with clean hearts and the promise of eternal life.

That's why we no longer rely on animal sacrifices like in ancient times—because Jesus fulfilled the very purpose they were pointing to. Those animal sacrifices were just a shadow—a temporary symbol pointing forward to something greater. Under the Old Testament, people followed specific laws and rituals to seek forgiveness and stay in right standing with God. But those rituals were never meant to be the final answer. They were like signposts, preparing the way for the ultimate solution: Jesus Christ. He is the reality those ancient practices were pointing to—the true and perfect sacrifice Who would deal with sin once and for all.

He is the spotless Lamb of God, the holy offering. He didn't just cover sin—He removed it completely for those who believe.

The beauty of the gospel is that it's not about religion or tradition—it's about a Person. And His invitation is for everyone.

God made a way. The veil that once separated humanity from His presence was torn, and through Jesus Christ, we now have full access to the Living God. No other offering is needed. Jesus is the fulfillment of everything our hearts have longed for: forgiveness, peace, inward transformation, and the promise of eternal life. He is the fulfillment of every ancient promise, every foreshadowing, and every longing for redemption.

This sacrificial blood of Jesus wasn't just for forgiveness of our sins or purifying our hearts—it's also our defense. You can **plead this blood of Jesus Christ** over yourself, your family, your home, your vehicle, your workplace—anywhere you sense the need for divine protection. If you've never done this before, here are some **simple and practical examples** of how to pray and use the name and blood of Jesus in your daily life:

- **When you feel fear or anxiety**, say out loud: "In the name of Jesus, I rebuke this fear. I cover my mind with the blood of Jesus Christ."
- **Before you go to sleep**, pray: "Holy Heavenly Father, in Jesus' name, I plead the blood of Christ over my dreams, my mind, and this home. Protect me from all darkness."
- **Over your children or loved ones**, say: "I plead the blood of Jesus over [name]. No weapon formed against them shall prosper. Protect them, guide them, and break every chain the enemy has tried to place on them." I claim Your protection over them, LORD. In the name of Jesus Christ. Amen."
- **When faced with temptation or attack**, declare: "I have been given authority through Jesus Christ. Devil,

I command you to flee in Jesus' name. I plead the blood over my heart, mind, and body."

- **For ongoing daily protection:** "I plead the blood of Jesus Christ over my mind, my body, my family, and everything You've entrusted to me. I claim Your protection and peace today. In Your Almighty name of Jesus Christ. Amen."

You don't need to be perfect or religious to use the name and blood of Jesus. You simply need to **believe in His power and speak it with faith**. His name works because He is alive. His blood still speaks because it is eternal. And when you align yourself with the truth of who Jesus is—and who you are in Him—you begin to walk in a power that the enemy cannot defeat. His name still works. His blood still protects. In Jesus Christ, you are fully armed. It's through His sacrifice and His authority that we can approach God with boldness. This is your inheritance as a child of God—**use it boldly**.

Earlier in this book, I shared a YouTube channel, ALL IN CHRIST, which offers uplifting worship songs for us believers. While singing and dancing are beautiful expressions of worship, they are just a few of the many ways we can honor God. Worship takes many forms, and some of the most powerful ways to worship include fasting combined with prayer and reading God's Word, or simply reading His Word daily, serving others with love and kindness, practicing generosity, offering thanksgiving to God in all circumstances, and praying for the salvation of others. As 1 Corinthians 10:31 (NIV) enlightens us, **"So whether you eat or drink or whatever you do, do it all for the glory of God."** Everything we do in life, from the simplest tasks to the most significant actions, can be an act of worship when we do it with the intention of honoring God. Just remember, the more worship we offer to God, the more blessings pour down upon us!

In this book, I won't delve deeply into the various types of worship, as that will come later. My primary goal right now is to help you experience the gift of salvation. Once you are saved, the true desire for worship—one that comes from the heart and the Holy Spirit—will naturally flow from within you. True worship is not something we can simply learn through rules or rituals; it is something the Holy Spirit cultivates in us after we receive Him as the eternal gift of salvation. As you grow in genuine faith, your understanding and expression of worship will deepen, and you will find that your life itself becomes a living offering to God.

In the end, the battle is real, but so is the power of prayer, worship, and the name of Jesus Christ. Through consistent prayer, we connect with the Almighty, strengthening our faith and standing firm against the enemy's attacks. Worship becomes a weapon, drawing us closer to God and refueling us for the battles ahead. And in His name, we find our ultimate protection and authority—authority to trample on the enemy's schemes, to speak life over ourselves and those we love, and to declare victory over every situation. Remember, the enemy has no power over you when you use the name of Jesus Christ; it is the name that makes demons tremble and forces of darkness flee. The more you understand the power of His name and blood, the more equipped you'll be to walk in victory every day. So, press on in prayer, stand firm in worship, and use the name of Jesus boldly—it is your weapon, your shield, and your ultimate victory.

Chapter 13

What Could Hinder or Delay Prayer Response?

When we pray, we often hope for a response, whether it's peace, guidance, or a change in our situation. We trust that our prayers will be heard, but sometimes it feels like they go unanswered. It can be confusing and frustrating when this happens, especially when we are truly seeking help or clarity. In this chapter, we will explore what might be preventing our prayers from receiving a response. There are a number of reasons that can get in the way, and understanding them can help us see things more clearly and improve the way we approach prayer.

One of the most important reasons prayers might not be answered is the absence of the Holy Spirit. For believers, the Holy Spirit plays a crucial role in prayer. Through the Holy Spirit, we have a direct connection to God, allowing us to communicate with Him in ways that go beyond our understanding. This connection makes a world of difference, as it accelerates the response to our prayers and helps us align our requests with God's will. The Bible confirms this truth: **"The prayer of a righteous person is powerful and effective"** (James 5:16, NIV). And we are made righteous (right with God)—not by our own efforts—but by the presence of the Holy Spirit within us, working through us, and bringing our prayers into harmony with the heart of God.

Without the Holy Spirit, that connection is missing; our prayers might not be as effective. If we're disconnected from this spiritual help, it becomes harder to receive the answers or peace we're seeking. This is not just a matter of belief but also of openness to the deeper spiritual communion that prayer requires. But when we are saved and receive the Holy Spirit, our communication with God becomes personal and direct— an incredible gift in itself!

Moreover, being saved through Jesus Christ means we are no longer burdened by shame and fear over our sins, because His blood has covered them all! This gives us confidence and freedom to approach God without fear. The Holy Spirit not only helps us communicate with God, but He also guides us to pray in alignment with God's will, helping us pray genuinely and wholeheartedly. It takes our prayer life and worship to an entirely new level. It is truly a blessing to be filled with God's Spirit because this connection with God through His Spirit is one of the greatest gifts we can experience. I wish everyone could experience this incredible blessing of salvation.

Another critical factor that can hinder the response to prayer is the interference of evil forces. There are tons of evil forces at work in the world that try to block or disrupt prayers. These unclean dark forces don't want us to receive answers, guidance, or support. If we imagine prayer as sending a message to a higher power, these evil forces can be like obstacles in the way, making it harder for that message to reach its destination. This is why persistence in prayer is so important. The enemy, whether in the form of doubt, fear, or external negativity, is often impatient, and it wants to stop you from receiving what you're asking for. If you give up too soon, you might never see the breakthrough that could be just around the corner. This is why a consistent and persistent prayer life is so valuable. We need to keep praying, even when it feels like nothing is happening.

Another reason prayers might not be answered is when we pray outside of God's will or at the wrong time. It's easy to ask for things that seem good to us, but not all of our desires align with what is best for us in the grand scheme of life. God has a unique plan for each person and an appointed time for everything. Sometimes, our prayers may not align with that plan or the timing He has set. This can be difficult to accept, especially when we're asking for something we really want. The idea is that prayers should be in line with what God has planned, and sometimes, even though we may feel strongly about our requests, the timing or the nature of those requests might not fit with what is best for us or others. Trusting that everything happens for a reason and that there is a Supreme order can help us find peace when our prayers don't seem to be answered immediately.

Beyond these larger spiritual dynamics, there are practical and personal factors that can affect our prayers. Lack of faith is one of the biggest hurdles. It's hard to believe in something you can't see or touch, but faith is an essential part of prayer. Faith is what turns prayer into a genuine conversation with our LORD, where we trust that what we ask for has the potential to come to pass. The Bible says it's impossible to please God without placing our faith in Him alone. Without faith or belief, we may struggle to see how our prayers could be answered, which may lead to doubt or discouragement.

But here's the thing—once you're filled with the Holy Spirit, something incredible happens. Your faith doesn't just stay the same; it deepens, almost automatically. Once you start experiencing real miracles and revelations—those undeniable moments that confirm the true power of Christ in your life—your faith grows exponentially. I can't even begin to express how profoundly these supernatural experiences have strengthened my faith since receiving salvation.

Let me be completely honest with you: there is **no way** my faith would've survived this long—especially through the rollercoaster of trials, meltdowns, and "Please, Jesus, take the wheel" moments—if it weren't for the countless supernatural encounters, the divine confirmations, and those Holy Spirit pep talks straight from Jesus Himself. Without those sacred check-ins, I'd be a spiritual puddle on the floor somewhere. And let's be real—this faith? It's not something I whipped up like a Pinterest recipe. It's a full-blown gift from the Holy Spirit. A **gift**. Because left to my own emotional chaos and overthinking? Yeah… I'd be curled up in a blanket fort with snacks, avoiding life entirely.

But in all seriousness, this faith isn't just a feel-good boost or emotional hype—it's real power. It empowers you to trust that God is truly present in your life, guiding you through every challenge and decision. As your faith grows, so does your ability to believe in the impossible. The power of prayer starts to feel tangible—like something you can reach out and grab. You begin to recognize God's hand at work, pulling you closer to His will and His purpose for your life. It's not just belief anymore; it becomes a living, breathing connection with the divine that transforms everything.

Unforgiveness is another powerful barrier to prayers' quick response. Holding on to grudges or hurt can cloud our ability to connect with our Almighty God, as well as distort our understanding of our true desires. If we are unwilling to forgive others, it is believed that this may block our ability to receive forgiveness or blessings ourselves. Letting go of bitterness is a crucial step in clearing the path for our prayers to be heard. It's not about the other person—it's about freeing ourselves from the weight of unforgiveness so that we can draw closer to God.

If you find it difficult to forgive someone and let go of the hurt, you can always ask God to help you with it. Not only does this aid in your healing, but it also aligns you with God's will for your life. God's will for all of us is to forgive one another, just as He forgives us. By praying for the strength to forgive, you are fulfilling His will and allowing His peace to flow into your life. In other words, you are surrendering to His will, which is a crucial step toward forgiveness and yielding to God's purpose. This was a turning point in my healing. I started praying for those who had hurt me, and I believe it played a key role in my salvation.

Only after I got saved, I later discovered in the Bible that this is exactly what we are called to do. We are called to pray for our enemies, as Jesus teaches in Matthew 5:44-45 (NIV): **"But I tell you, love your enemies and pray for those who persecute you, that you may be children of Your Father in heaven."** At the time, I was practicing this intuitively, simply because it made me feel better. I was very lonely and had no one to talk to about my problems, so all I had left was to pour out my grief, resentments, and hurt to God in prayer. Looking back, it's evident that this practice of praying for others became a turning point in my journey toward both healing and salvation.

In the same way, the love we show to God—through actions like love and forgiveness—is the only true "currency" in His eyes. In heaven, love is the most valuable thing we can offer. The more love you have for those around you, the richer you are in God's eyes—because when you show love to people, you show God to people. It's not the wealth, fame, or power we accumulate on earth, but the love we pour out on others that determines our true spiritual richness. Jesus makes this clear when He says in Luke 7:47 (NIV), **"Therefore, I tell you, her many sins have been forgiven—as her great love has shown. But whoever has been forgiven little loves little."** The opposite is also true: those who forgive much, love much. This powerful truth reminds us that love and forgiveness go hand in hand.

When we love, we forgive—even if that forgiveness needs to be extended daily. In Matthew 18:21-22 (NKJV), Peter asks Jesus, **"LORD, how often shall my brother sin against me, and I forgive him? Up to seven times?"** To which Jesus replies, **"I do not say to you, up to seven times, but up to seventy times seven."** Jesus' words call us to forgive endlessly, without keeping track, just as He forgives all our sins—past, present, and future—and does not hold them against us. This illustrates that forgiveness is not a one-time act but a continuous choice, rooted in love and compassion. By forgiving, we reflect God's boundless grace, opening our hearts to the power of love, which heals, restores, frees us from the burden of unforgiveness, and ultimately leads us to salvation.

You've likely heard many times that we must forgive quickly, letting go of bitterness and choosing to love one another as we love ourselves. Love is what conquers all, they say. But do we truly understand why? It's much easier to hold onto anger or choose not to forgive. In doing so, we might feel justified in our hurt, but why should we forgive? Why love? What's the point? After all, it's easier to stay in the position of the victim, to nurture our grievances.

The answer is simple: the enemy cannot do anything against it—he cannot win when we choose love and forgiveness. The enemy hates love and forgiveness! These are not just good moral choices; they are powerful **spiritual weapons** against these evil forces. Love and forgiveness directly oppose the devil's strategy to divide, deceive, and destroy. Every time we choose to forgive, we tear down his schemes and shut the door to his influence. But when we choose to hold on to bitterness, resentment, or unforgiveness, we unknowingly open a door to the enemy. Jesus even warned in Matthew 18:34–35 that unforgiveness invites tormentors—demonic forces—into our lives. These evil entities gain a **legal right** in the spiritual realm to harass and torment us because unforgiveness creates a stronghold in our hearts and minds.

Yes! There are rules and laws in the spiritual realm as well—just like there are in the physical. Believe it or not, even demons—our accusers—are bound by spiritual laws. They cannot just do whatever they want; they need permission or a legal right to access certain areas of our lives. And when we hold on to unforgiveness, we unknowingly grant them that access. When we refuse to forgive, we step out from under the covering of God's grace and protection—leaving ourselves vulnerable to spiritual attacks like anxiety, anger, fear, confusion, and even physical affliction.

But the moment we choose to forgive, we break their legal claim. We close the door and cancel their assignment in Jesus' name. Forgiveness isn't just about healing relationships—it's about spiritual freedom. Forgiveness breaks the chains. And in doing so, we allow the Holy Spirit to flood our hearts with peace, healing, and restoration.

When we choose forgiveness, we break that hold and deny the enemy any foothold in our lives. We take away his power to manipulate, divide, or sow discord. More than just words, your actions of love and forgiveness **declare your allegiance to God**, not to the forces of darkness. You make a powerful statement that you are **on the side of good**, aligned with God's will to bring peace, healing, and restoration. And in doing so, you not only protect your heart from harm but also align yourself with God's perfect plan of reconciliation, embodying His love and grace in a broken world.

As Romans 12:21 (NIV) says, **"Do not be overcome by evil, but overcome evil with good."** By choosing love and forgiveness, you take a stand against the enemy's attacks and overcome them with the goodness of God's love. Do not give the enemy any opportunity to gain victory in your life. Choose love. Choose forgiveness. Remember: **When you show love to people, you show God to people.** In doing so, you declare before heaven and earth that you stand firm in the light of His truth—and that no weapon formed against you shall prosper. Do not allow the enemy to win this spiritual battle. Let love guide your decisions, for truly, love conquers all.

And remember, as Romans 12:19 (NIV) further teaches us, **"Do not take revenge, my dear friends, but leave room for God's wrath, for it is written: 'It is Mine to avenge; I will repay,' says the LORD."** The LORD's justice is perfect! He will not let anyone get away with anything. Trust that God will handle the injustices in your life. It may not happen right when you want it, but rest assured, it will unfold according to His perfect timing. For now, when you choose forgiveness, you leave room for His justice to work, releasing your desire for vengeance and allowing His perfect will to unfold in your life. So, I encourage you, my beloved, to take that step of faith— **choose to be better, not bitter.** Ask God to help you to forgive those who have hurt you, surrender your pain to Him, and watch as His healing power transforms your heart, brings you closer to the peace only He can provide, and ultimately leads you to salvation.

Sin in our lives can also delay answers to our prayers. When we live in ways that go against our faith and values, it creates a barrier between us and God. This doesn't mean we need to be perfect, but recognizing where we fall short and striving to live with integrity can open the door for God to answer our prayers and ultimately bring us to salvation. We do not strive for perfection; we strive to rely on God's almighty power to transform and renew us. Sin—big or small—creates separation from Him, making it harder to connect with God in prayer. It is only through honest reflection and admitting our sins that we can align our hearts with God and pray in a way that draws us closer to Him.

God's greatest desire is for us to recognize our need for the unlimited power of Jesus Christ, our Savior. In His deep love, He is always ready to draw us near, gently guiding us toward repentance and renewal. As we humbly admit our shortcomings, God takes the lead in forgiving, restoring, and transforming us. When we recognize our flaws and bring them before our Holy Heavenly Father, it shows Him that we are maturing spiritually. By acknowledging our sins, we demonstrate our willingness to grow in faith and obedience, and God sees in us a heart ready for deeper communion with

Him. This is a significant step toward spiritual maturity. God is at work in our hearts, preparing us for His calling and patiently waiting for us to become spiritually mature—ready to fully embrace our identity as His adopted children and step into the fullness of His love and grace.

So, run to our loving Heavenly Father with all honesty, admitting that you need His help. He is always there, ready to embrace you and provide what you need. Do not rely on your own strength to transform yourself—rather, trust in God's power to change you from the inside out. Only He has the power to bring true transformation. We cannot do it on our own. We cannot rely on our strength to become a better person—true transformation comes **only through His unlimited power**. We are not capable of doing it on our own. All He asks is for your willingness to change, and He will take care of the rest. Trust in His ability to transform you, not in your own efforts. Simply ask Him for help, remain persistent, and He will provide all that you need.

Pride, self-centered motives, and failure to seek God first can also create obstacles in our prayer life. If our prayers are selfish or designed to elevate our position, rather than seeking the good of others or a higher purpose, they may not be answered as we hope. Prayer is not just about asking for things for ourselves, but about aligning with a greater purpose—whether it's forgiveness, peace, or helping others. When our motives are pure and focused on something beyond our benefit, we're more likely to see meaningful responses.

Finally, a lack of perseverance can hinder prayers' responses. Sometimes, the answers don't come right away. It can take time, patience, and persistence to see the results. In our fast-paced world, we often want immediate results, but prayer is not always about quick fixes. It requires a willingness to wait, trust, and continue seeking answers, even when things seem uncertain. Our patient Heavenly Father wants to see our effort and persistence. Perseverance in prayer is a sign of faith and trust that, even though we don't see immediate results, the process of prayer itself is valuable and meaningful.

In conclusion, if you're not yet saved, the key to unlocking faster and more powerful prayer responses is being filled with the Holy Spirit. Without the Holy Spirit, you are missing the crucial connection to God that accelerates your prayers on a whole new level. Through salvation, not only are your sins forgiven, but you also gain direct access to God, who will guide you to pray in alignment with His will and navigate life's challenges. It's important to understand that prayer isn't just about asking for what we want, but about aligning ourselves with God's perfect plan. Sin, unforgiveness, doubt, and selfish motives can all hinder prayer responses, but when you turn to God in faith and repentance, He will fill you with His Spirit, transforming both your heart and your prayers. If you're seeking answers, guidance, or peace through prayer but aren't seeing results, I urge you to prioritize being filled with the Holy Spirit above all else. The Holy Spirit is the key to unlocking more powerful and immediate responses to your prayers. Once you are saved, your communication with God becomes personal, and your prayers will bear fruit in ways you never imagined. The Holy Spirit is the answer to faster, more effective prayer responses!

Chapter 14

Divine Protection: Saved from a Car Accident

Even after I encountered salvation and witnessed undeniable proof of God's presence in my life, I still wrestled with moments of doubt. The enemy whispered lies that it was all in my head—that maybe I had only imagined God's hand at work. That what I believed to be divine guidance was nothing more than coincidence or imagination. But God, in His mercy, went even further to reassure me. He confirmed that I wasn't losing my mind. Everything I was experiencing truly was part of His divine plan. And He used one of the most unexpected, beautiful vessels to do it: my two-year-old daughter, Sophia.

God began speaking through her in ways that were undeniable. Multiple times, He used her innocent voice to confirm things I had already sensed through visions and promptings from the Holy Spirit. These were not general feelings or vague impressions—these were direct, timely, and Spirit-filled confirmations. One particular moment still gives me chills to this day.

I had just picked Sophia up from daycare. As usual, I stopped at a stop sign near her daycare and turned to ask her about her day. Normally, she'd smile and babble back a few words. But this time was different. She didn't look at me at all. Her beautiful little face stayed fixed straight ahead, completely serious, and then she said, "Watch the road."

At first, I was taken aback. As I began to make a left turn, again she said, "Watch the road." A third time, with even more urgency, she repeated it. It was as if she were overcome by a power beyond her natural awareness. In that instant, a sudden supernatural knowing dropped into my spirit. I knew a white truck was going to come speeding toward us. I hadn't seen anything yet, but the Holy Spirit impressed that knowledge into me with such clarity and force that I instinctively hit the brakes to slow down.

And sure enough, just seconds later, as I began to cautiously inch forward, a white truck came flying out of an alley from behind a building, where neither of us could have seen it coming. It raced right in front of us where we would have been if I hadn't slowed down. There was no warning, no screeching tires, no sound at all until it was already barreling past. If I had kept going, we would have been hit directly.

I gripped the steering wheel and let out a shaky breath. My heart pounded, but in the midst of the fear was also awe. I knew without a shadow of a doubt: this was a divine intervention. It was as if Heaven reached down, wrapped us in protection, and shielded us in that split second. God used my daughter's voice to grab my attention, to pierce through distraction, and to warn me before danger arrived. And through that, He reminded me that I was not alone, not crazy, not imagining things. I was hearing Him—and He was near.

This wasn't the only time God used Sophia to alert me, affirm His word, or remind me of His presence—as you'll discover later in this book. Over time, I began to see a pattern—not just moments of grace, but a lifestyle of divine care. I started to realize something powerful: as a follower of Christ, filled with the Holy Spirit, I was walking under His protection. And so was my daughter! The enemy could try to plant seeds of doubt, but the voice of God always speaks louder—sometimes even through the lips of a child.

What makes this even more incredible is how consistent this is with the heart of God in Scripture. Jesus said in Matthew 18:3 (NIV), **"Truly I tell you, unless you change and become like little children, you will never enter the Kingdom of Heaven."** Children are not only cherished by God—they are often the clearest vessels of His voice because of their innocence, their humility, and their openness to trust.

And again, in Matthew 21:16 (NIV), Jesus confirms the sacred role of children when He quotes Psalm 8: **"From the lips of children and infants you, LORD, have called forth your praise."** In doing so, He affirms that even the smallest and most dependent voices are not only heard by God—they are **ordained to declare His glory**. God doesn't need powerful titles or lofty platforms to move; He delights in using the humble, the overlooked, and the pure-hearted to carry His power and purpose. My daughter Sophia, though only two years old, became a **living testimony** of this truth. In her innocence, she carried a divine message—one that cut through doubt and fear, reminding me that God is not only real, but intimately near.

It reminded me of how God used the boy Samuel in the Old Testament. In 1 Samuel 3 (NIV), the young child heard God calling his name while he was lying in bed. Though he didn't understand at first, eventually, he responded with the words, **"Speak, LORD, for your servant is listening."** Children also can hear God. They can respond to Him. And sometimes, they deliver heaven's most important messages to us. In that moment, Sophia wasn't just my daughter—she was a messenger.

After that encounter, I began to live with a new awareness. I paid more attention to the small nudges, to the sudden insights, and yes—even to the random words spoken by children. I realized God's voice isn't always dramatic or loud. Sometimes, it's as gentle as a child's warning in a quiet car ride home. Our job is to stay tuned in. To listen. To not dismiss the small signs, because sometimes, they're the most powerful of all.

So if you're reading this and wondering whether God still speaks—He does. If you're unsure whether He still protects—He absolutely does. And if you've doubted whether you're capable of hearing His voice—let this be your reminder: He can use anyone. Even you. Even your child. Even the most unlikely vessel.

God is not limited by age, status, or circumstance. God is limitless. He's looking for open hearts. Hearts that trust. Hearts that listen. Hearts that say, **"Speak, LORD. I'm here. I am listening."**

That day in the car changed how I listen. It changed how I trust. And it reminded me that no matter what the world says, no matter what doubt whispers, God is always near. Always speaking. Always protecting.

Chapter 15

More of Divine Revelations: Supernatural Visions

These revelations from God did not stop with the initial vision I shared at the beginning of this book. To my astonishment, I continued to experience more and more visions in the days that followed. The first two years of my salvation have been overflowing with miraculous moments and divine encounters—there are so many, it's almost overwhelming to capture them all here.

Even sharing just a few of these visions feels remarkable, as each one holds incredible significance. After all, we're talking about revelations from the Supreme God Himself! To receive even a single vision from Him is a blessing beyond measure. Yet, He has granted me multiple, confirming His existence and love to someone as unworthy as myself. The sheer abundance of these visions fills me with awe, and I am humbled to share the most profound among them with you, as that is what God calls us to do as born-again believers in Christ.

We are called to share the miraculous, the supernatural, and the truth of His existence with a world that is often so blind and asleep to it—just as I once was. These experiences are not merely stories; they are sacred testimonies to the reality of God and His active, loving presence. As it says in Matthew 10:32-33 (NKJV): **"Therefore whoever confesses Me before men, him I will also confess before My Father Who is in heaven. But whoever denies Me before men,** him I will also deny before My Father Who is in heaven."

Similarly, in Mark 8:38 (NIV): **"If anyone is ashamed of Me and My words in this adulterous and sinful generation, the Son of Man will be ashamed of them when He comes in His Father's glory with the holy angels."** This is why it is so important for us to speak boldly, despite any fear or opposition that tries to silence us, because we are called to stand firm in our faith and acknowledge God's truth before the world. The time has come to share what has been revealed, without hesitation, and to lead others to the life-changing reality of God's Kingdom and eternal life in heaven.

Jesus Himself instructed us to go into all the world and preach the Gospel (Mark 16:15). Paul reminds us that the love of Christ compels us because we know that Jesus died for all of us (2 Corinthians 5:14). So, as I share the next visions, know that this isn't just about my journey; it's about fulfilling a **divine mission** to bring the reality of God's Kingdom closer to everyone willing to listen. God desires all to be saved and to come to the knowledge of the truth (1 Timothy 2:4). Stop seeking the truth elsewhere. God's ultimate truth is here; it's real, and it's meant for everyone.

Chapter 16

Golden Field of Wheat

At the beginning of my journey with visions and revelations, I saw a vast golden field of wheat, fully ripe and ready for harvest. This field was not just a beautiful sight; it was a powerful symbol indicating that the time for reaping was upon us. Just as a harvest requires timely labor, this vision reminded me that souls are waiting to be reached, lives yearning for the truth, and hearts longing for the love of Christ.

The harvest is plentiful, and God desires His people to step into their calling as laborers, to gather in the lost and the broken, sharing the good news of salvation. As Jesus said in Matthew 9:37, **"The harvest is plentiful but the workers are few,"** it is a powerful statement of the urgent need for workers in God's field. It reinforces the importance of being vigilant and responsive, for the fields around us are bursting with potential. Each stalk of wheat represents individuals whose lives could be transformed through the love and truth of Christ.

God is inviting us to join Him in this great harvest, reminding us that He equips us with everything we need to fulfill our purpose. It is a time of great expectation, a season where His Kingdom is advancing, and we are privileged to be a part of it. This vision encourages us to embrace our roles in the divine plan, actively engaging in the work of the Kingdom and trusting that God will provide growth and increase as we labor faithfully in His name.

Chapter 17

Rocket Launching

The next vision I'd like to share is of a rocket launch—an unmistakable symbol of new beginnings and explosive growth. At that time, it suggested that God was propelling me into a new phase of my journey, one marked by momentum and purpose. Just as a rocket is launched with force to reach heights it could never attain on its own; this vision indicated that God was moving me beyond previous limitations and into a season of significant transformation. The rocket signified acceleration, pointing to changes that would be both swift and impactful. Finally!

In that moment, God revealed to me that He was fueling me with His power to reach spiritual heights I had not anticipated. Like a rocket launch, which is meticulously planned and precisely timed, God had prepared me for this moment—aligning circumstances and experiences to propel me forward. This vision affirmed that He was launching me into a purpose divinely designed and predestined, with Him guiding the entire journey. From that point on, my faith skyrocketed in astonishing ways! Hallelujah! Praise our LORD God Almighty!

Chapter 18

Drowning Boy Saved by Jesus. Gifts

One particularly striking prophetic vision deeply moved my heart: I saw a boy with short blonde hair and bright blue eyes, wearing a blue-collared T-shirt, drowning in a pool. Imagine my astonishment when, later, I turned on the TV and saw that very boy, now miraculously rescued by Jesus Himself! The scene was breathtaking, with Jesus depicted reaching out His hand to save him. To top it all off, the brave boy even drew a poignant picture of that miraculous moment—Jesus embracing him after the rescue! The joy of witnessing such a divine intervention left me in awe, reinforcing my faith in the power of God's love and the reality of His active presence and salvation in our lives.

In the same vision of the drowning boy, immediately afterward, I saw my coffee table covered with numerous gifts—blue boxes scattered across the table and spilling onto the floor. The vision ended with a countdown: 2...1. The abundance of blue gifts in the vision reminded me of divine packages—supernatural gifts that God gives to His people through the Holy Spirit. These are not merely natural talents, but powerful spiritual empowerments intended to strengthen the body of Christ and advance His Kingdom here on earth. These gifts are meant to be used for the common good, to glorify God, and to draw others closer to Him. Each gift is a manifestation of God's presence and power through the Holy Spirit, dwelling in saved believers, offering a way to be actively involved in His redemptive work and to testify to the world of God's power.

One of the most evident manifestations is the **working of miracles** (1 Corinthians 12:10). Miracles, as signs and wonders, demonstrate God's divine intervention in the natural world, often bringing healing, deliverance, or supernatural provision. **Prophecy** is another vital gift of the Spirit (1 Corinthians 12:10), enabling believers to speak forth God's will, provide encouragement, and warn or direct others according to His purposes.

The **gift of healing** (1 Corinthians 12:9) is also a powerful manifestation, bringing restoration to physical, emotional, and spiritual ailments. Likewise, the **word of knowledge** (1 Corinthians 12:8) and **word of wisdom** (1 Corinthians 12:8) are gifts that equip believers with supernatural insight—knowledge of things not learned naturally, and wisdom to apply that knowledge in godly ways. **The gift of faith** (1 Corinthians 12:9), distinct from saving faith, empowers believers to trust God in extraordinary circumstances, believing in the impossible.

Tongues and **the interpretation of tongues** (1 Corinthians 12:10, 14:13) are spiritual gifts that allow believers to communicate with God in a heavenly language, building up their faith and, when interpreted, edifying the church. Another essential manifestation is the **discerning of spirits** (1 Corinthians 12:10), which allows believers to distinguish between the influence of the Holy Spirit and evil spirits, helping to protect the body of Christ from deceptions.

Additionally, the Holy Spirit equips believers with practical gifts that serve to strengthen the church and extend the kingdom of God. **Helps** (1 Corinthians 12:28) refers to the gift of serving others, often behind the scenes, with humility and dedication. **Administration** (1 Corinthians 12:28) provides leadership in organizing church activities and ensuring that the work of the ministry runs smoothly. The **gift of teaching** (Romans 12:7) enables believers to accurately convey God's word, helping others grow in understanding. **Leadership** (Romans 12:8) is the gift to guide and direct others in their spiritual walk, often involving vision and pastoral care. **Encouragement** (Romans 12:8), or exhortation, enables believers to offer comfort, challenge, and spiritual support to others, helping them persevere in their faith.

Lastly, the Holy Spirit gives **ministry gifts** (Ephesians 4:11-13), which include apostles, prophets, evangelists, pastors, and teachers, each playing a vital role in equipping the saints for the work of the ministry and the building up of the body of Christ. These gifts are essential for the church's growth and maturity, enabling believers to fulfill their calling and impact the world for Christ.

As we reflect on these gifts, it's essential to understand that all of them come from the same Holy Spirit, who distributes them according to His will. 1 Corinthians 12:11 (NIV) tells us, **"All these are the work of One and the same Spirit, and He distributes them to each one, just as He determines."** No one can predict how many gifts we will receive or when they will manifest, but one thing is certain: every gift is given for the common good and to empower believers to fulfill Christ's mission on earth. In His perfect timing, the Holy Spirit equips us with the gifts needed to accomplish His purpose for our lives.

As believers, we are invited to actively participate in the expansion of God's Kingdom on earth through the use of these gifts. The tremendous privilege of operating in the gifts of the Spirit is not just for our benefit but to bless others and bring them closer to God's love and truth. Whether it's through healing, prophecy, miracles, or any other spiritual gift, we are called to be vessels of His power and presence, demonstrating His love in tangible ways. What an incredible honor it is to be entrusted with these divine gifts, knowing that we are participating in the ongoing work of redemption and reconciliation in the world. Through these gifts, we become active participants in the unfolding of God's Kingdom here on earth, partnering with Him in His work to bring healing, restoration, and transformation to the world around us. Ultimately, the gifts are given to **glorify God**, not ourselves, reflecting His grace and power through believers, so that others may be drawn to Him by the power of the Holy Spirit.

Chapter 19

The Supreme Gift: Love Above All Spiritual Gifts

In the realm of spiritual gifts and manifestations of God's Spirit, one truth stands as the foundation upon which everything else is built: love is the greatest gift of all. While spiritual gifts such as prophecy, healing, and wisdom are undeniably powerful, they pale in comparison to the transformative and unifying force of love. As the Apostle Paul teaches us in 1 Corinthians 13:1-3 (NIV), **"If I speak in the tongues of men or of angels, but do not have love, I am only a resounding gong or a clanging cymbal. If I have the gift of prophecy and can fathom all mysteries and all knowledge, and if I have a faith that can move mountains, but do not have love, I am nothing. If I give all I possess to the poor and give over my body to hardship that I may boast, but do not have love, I gain nothing."**

These verses clearly illustrate that, no matter how many gifts we may possess, they mean nothing without love. Spiritual gifts are powerful, but they are empty and ineffective without the foundation of love. Paul continues in 1 Corinthians 13:13 (NIV), **"And now these three remain: faith, hope, and love. But the greatest of these is love."**

Love binds all other gifts together and reflects God's very nature. In Galatians 5:22-23, love is listed first among the fruits of the Spirit, reinforcing that it's foundational to all other virtues. True love is sacrificial, patient, and kind, mirroring God's love for us. Without love, our actions, however noble they may appear, are hollow and disconnected from the heart of God.

It's essential to pray for an increase in love, asking God to fill us with His perfect love and to help us grow in our ability to love others. In 1 John 4:16 (NIV), it says, **"God is love. Whoever lives in love lives in God, and God in them."** We should regularly pray to embody this love—asking the LORD to help us love more deeply, more selflessly, and more fully, so that His love flows through us into every relationship and moment. Love transcends all other gifts and serves as the ultimate reflection of God's character in our lives, nurturing our hearts to embody the very essence of Christ's teachings. So never underestimate its power. Let me say it again: **when you show love to people, you show God to people.**

Chapter 20

The Arm of the LORD Revealed

It was around this time that God revealed His arm to me through Michelangelo's iconic painting, "Creation of Adam." The artwork vividly illustrated the profound connection between God and humanity, reinforcing the truth that we are created to be in a relationship with Him.

The masterpiece, painted on the ceiling of the Sistine Chapel, depicts God reaching out to touch the finger of Adam, igniting life and offering a profound connection between the Creator and His creation. Michelangelo, a man of deep faith, was profoundly inspired, and this painting is often regarded as a spiritual expression of God's divine touch and His intimate desire for a relationship with humanity. The artwork portrays not only the creation of life but also the moment of divine grace—the very arm of God extended to humanity, inviting us to partake in His eternal love and life.

The arm of the LORD represents God's power and intervention in our lives. The proximity of the hands, almost but not quite touching, reflects the gap between humanity's sin and God's holiness. This gap is ultimately bridged by Jesus Christ, our only Savior, as part of the divine plan for redemption. Michelangelo's painting, though created centuries ago, serves as a beautiful artistic interpretation of this spiritual truth, echoing God's eternal desire to offer life and personal connection between Him and His creation.

Later, I came across Isaiah chapter 53, verse 1 (NIV), which asked the most important question in the world: **"Who has believed our message and to whom has the arm of the LORD been revealed?"** This question cut to the very heart of God's plan of salvation, and as I meditated on it, I was struck by the magnitude of its significance. The phrase 'the arm of the LORD' serves as a powerful metaphor, symbolizing God's might, His divine intervention, and, ultimately, the salvation He offers through the gift of eternal life in Paradise. It speaks of the unmistakable revelation of God's power to save, to redeem, and to give life. The 'arm of the LORD' refers to the unveiling of God's saving power through the suffering of the Servant—Jesus Christ—who bore our sins, offering Himself as the ultimate sacrifice for humanity's redemption.

What is truly awe-inspiring is the deeper meaning behind the word *LORD*, in all caps, as it replaces the original Hebrew name *YHVH*. In ancient Hebrew, *YHVH* carries a profound significance that can be broken down into two parts: **"Look for the Hand and look for the Nail."** When you look for the Hand and the Nail, you see the very essence of God's salvation. The Hand represents God's action, His intervention in the world, and the Nail points directly to the crucifixion of Jesus Christ, where God's plan of salvation was fully revealed. The imagery is so powerful—it is a divine blueprint, a message that calls all of humanity to witness the sacrifice of Christ on the cross as the ultimate expression of God's saving grace. And when we see it, when we recognize the Hand and the Nail, we understand that salvation has truly come—not just to Israel, but to the entire world today!

This revelation of *YHVH* echoes throughout the entire Bible, spanning both the Old and New Testaments, and is used nearly 7,000 times. The repetition of *YHVH* in the sacred writings is a constant, resounding reminder of God's unwavering commitment to bring salvation to His people. It is a message that transcends time, reverberating through the ages with the assurance of God's love and redemptive power. As the scriptures unfold, we see this promise of salvation played out, culminating in the life, death, and resurrection of Jesus Christ, whose sacrifice on the cross is the ultimate fulfillment of God's covenant with His people.

In this sacred name *YHVH*, we are reminded that salvation is not something we can earn, but a gift of grace, available to all who look to the Hand and the Nail with eyes of faith and repentant hearts that trust in God's eternal promises. The magnitude of this truth is overwhelming: God's salvation is a gift offered to the whole world, available to anyone who believes. When we look upon Christ's sacrifice, we are not merely witnessing an event in history, but we are encountering the living God who reached out in love to save us from hell. It's the wondrous, awe-filled truth that has been echoed through the centuries, resounding in every corner of the Earth. And it is in this revelation—the hand, the nail, and the salvation—that we find our hope, our redemption, and our eternal life.

This vision and verse really highlight that God's saving arm isn't just a metaphor—it's a real, active presence. It's His invitation for us to be reconciled and saved, a pursuit that started in the Garden of Eden and continues today. God calls each of us into His loving embrace, just as He reached out to Adam in the beginning. He's always extending His hand to guide, protect, and save us. In this powerful vision, I saw clearly that God's saving arm is always there for anyone willing to receive it, embracing us exactly as we are.

Chapter 21

The Snake

As I was praying and seeking answers for the coming year, I suddenly saw the back of a snake. In that moment, our Heavenly Father revealed to me the hidden workings of the enemy, exposing the dangers that were silently waiting to strike in the spiritual realm. It was as though He pulled back the curtain to show me the forces of darkness operating behind the scenes—waiting for an opportunity to deceive and attack. To my surprise, as soon as the snake noticed that I was observing it, it turned around, as startled to see me as I was to see it. Its eyes were disturbingly human-like, but filled with a pure, malevolent evil. The moment it realized I had caught sight of it, it lunged at me, its mouth wide open in a horrifying display of aggression. The sheer terror of the sight sent a surge of fear through me, causing me to quickly open my eyes in shock.

Despite the fear that gripped me in that moment, I was instantly back in my room, enveloped in the safety and peace of God's presence. His protection was immediate and undeniable, and I knew that He had not only shielded me from the attack but also shown me a glimpse of the enemy's schemes. In that instant, I understood that God had exposed the works of the devil to me, revealing how the enemy operates in the shadows, waiting for the right moment to strike. But now, with God's intervention, I saw the truth of its schemes laid bare. This powerful revelation reminded me that our Holy Father is always watching over His faithful children, alerting us to the dangers we cannot see, and protecting us from the enemy's traps. The enemy may still try to use deception and fear, but God is faithful in exposing his tactics and safeguarding His children from harm.

Shortly after this vision, I received a powerful confirmation from God: **"The LORD will fight for you, and you shall hold your peace."** This message echoed the truth that God stands against the forces of darkness on our behalf, just as He did for the Israelites in Exodus 14:14 (NKJV). In that moment, I learned that He would continue to shield and fight for us when we turn to Him in faith. As we stay vigilant and trust in His presence, God promises to be our defender, offering His supernatural peace and protection in every battle we face.

This encounter taught me a valuable lesson: seeking God for answers and guidance in our lives is a crucial practice to establish. By doing so, we are often warned before danger strikes, with God exposing the works of the devil so that we are not caught off guard. Through this, He reassures us that we have nothing to fear, for He is our constant protector, watching over us every step of the way.

Chapter 22

Through the Bird's Eye View

One beautiful morning, a remarkable experience unfolded as my two-year-old daughter began to share a collection of words and phrases that seemed completely nonsensical at the time. As the day went on, however, I realized that she had unwittingly provided me with an exact order of events that were occurring that very day! It was as if she had tapped into a divine current, and I was just beginning to understand the significance of her innocent utterances.

Later that same day, as the sunshine poured in through the windows, a vision washed over me. Suddenly, I found myself soaring through the air, seeing the world from a bird's eye view! I was gliding over familiar red rooftops, reminiscent of those in Arizona, and everything felt exhilarating. The vibrant landscape beneath me was alive, pulsating with energy. Then, in a moment of startling clarity, the bird's eye came right before me, reminding me of the beauty of perspective and the incredible heights to which God can lift us.

Just as the vision enveloped me, my daughter's voice rang out: "Look, mommy, look! There's a bird outside!" I rushed to the window, and there it was—a stunning bird perched in our backyard, a confirmation of what I had just experienced. In that instant, I realized that God was using my daughter to grab my attention, reassuring me amidst the doubts that the enemy had been trying to sow in my heart. It was as if God was saying through His creation, "I see you, I hear you, and I am with you!"

This moment was especially significant because God knows us better than we know ourselves. He understood the deep connection I have with my daughter, and He also knew that my love for birds would make the experience all the more meaningful. It was a personal touch from God, a beautiful reminder that He understands our hearts and uses the things that resonate with us to reveal His presence in personal ways.

Yet again, this was a strong confirmation that I am not insane, delivered through the purity and innocence of my daughter, Sophia. God knows us better than we know ourselves, and He knows exactly what means to use to approach each of us individually, in ways that will have an undeniable impact. Time and again, He has shown me His love through her, reminding me of the profound connection between divine guidance and the simplicity of a child's heart.

God's constant reassurance and comfort were undeniable, each vision strengthening my confidence and deepening my trust in His presence. He was making it clear that I was never meant to return to my old broken self, for His love and grace had transformed me. How unbelievably incredible is our LORD God?! This experience solidified my belief that God was guiding my journey, affirming that His presence was woven into the very fabric of my daily life. As I reflected on this vision, I felt an exhilarating sense of purpose and determination to embrace all that He had in store for me and my daughter. Each moment, each vision, was a step closer to the truth of His existence and the depth of His love.

Chapter 23

Family of Turtles

As I continued to receive revelations of God's undeniable existence, my mind buzzed with questions. I spent countless hours trying to unravel the mysteries of how God operates and how evil fits into the grand tapestry of life. I wrestled with the "how," "why," and "what" of it all, grappling with my limited understanding. Then, one day, God showed me a vision of a large turtle with baby turtles, all making their way to the water. The image felt very familiar and resonated deeply within me.

Later that day, a friend sent me a video to watch, completely unaware of the vision I had just received. To my astonishment, the video featured the same scene of a family of turtles embarking on their journey to the sea, accompanied by the story of Job from the Old Testament.

For those who may not be familiar, Job was a real man whose story is recorded in the Bible. He was known for his deep faith and integrity, even in the face of extreme suffering. Job's story teaches us that we can't always understand the full scope of God's infinite wisdom and sovereignty, and yet we are called to trust in His plan, regardless of our circumstances. As it states in Isaiah 55:8-9 (NIV), **"For My thoughts are not your thoughts, neither are your ways My ways," declares the LORD. "As the heavens are higher than the earth, so are My ways higher than your ways and My thoughts than your thoughts."** These verses encapsulate the essence of God's infinite wisdom. While pondering the intricacies of life, I was reminded that even the simple journey of turtles is under His sovereign control, and I am called to accept that God's ways are always higher than our ways.

Through Job's story, I learned that evil constantly seeks to accuse us before God, much like the adversary tried to challenge Job's integrity. Satan didn't just cause Job to suffer—he orchestrated every attack with one goal: to make Job curse God and turn away from Him. One by one, Job lost everything—his wealth, his children, and his health. But the attacks didn't stop there. Satan even used Job's own wife to tempt him, telling him to "curse God and die." Even Job's closest friends, instead of offering comfort, wrongly accused him of sin. They were mistakenly convinced that his suffering was a punishment from God.

Satan's tactic was clear: if he could make Job bitter, hopeless, or angry enough, maybe Job would rebel against God. But Job, though confused and brokenhearted, refused to do so. He grieved, he questioned, he cried out—but he never cursed God or abandoned his faith and love for Him. Despite everything, Job held on to his love and reverence for the LORD. And because of that, **satan lost**.

Job's story shows us that the enemy often tries to break us by using pain, loss, or even the voices of those around us. The goal is always the same—to separate us from God by stirring anger, doubt, or rebellion in our hearts. But Job proved that it's possible to endure even the hardest trials without turning away from God. His unwavering faith was a powerful testimony that **true love for God** isn't based on blessings, comfort, or favorable circumstances, but on a deep and genuine relationship with the One Who created us. In the end, God honored Job and restored everything he had lost—and even more. As it says in Job 42:10 (NIV), **"After Job had prayed for his friends, the LORD restored his fortunes and gave him twice as much as he had before."** This showed that no scheme of the enemy can overcome a heart fully surrendered to Him. Job's story is more than inspirational—it's a reminder of what faith can look like at its purest.

Job's perseverance and love for God reveal something essential: even when we don't understand what God is doing, we are still called to trust Him. His story reminds us that faith isn't about having all the answers—it's about trusting in God's goodness, especially when life doesn't make sense. We're not meant to unravel every mystery of good and evil, but to rely on our holy and loving Creator, Who sees the full picture and never leaves us alone in our suffering.

When difficult times arise, it's tempting to question God's intentions, especially when we don't immediately see the good in our situation. When trials come, it's easy to feel overwhelmed and question God's goodness. But we must resist this temptation to blame or doubt Him. After all, that is exactly what satan wants us to do!

Sometimes, it can take years to recognize how God was working behind the scenes for our ultimate good. So, I am learning not to stress over trying to figure everything out—God's ways are higher than ours, and His wisdom is beyond our comprehension (Isaiah 55:8-9). Instead, we need patience and faith in the Sovereign plan of God, knowing that He will bring about His good purposes in His perfect timing. As we endure trials, we must trust that God will align all things with His divine plan.

Think about Romans 8:28 (NIV) for a moment: **"And we know that in all things God works for the good of those who love Him..."** Even when life throws us curveballs, or things don't go the way we expect, we don't have to live in fear or worry. Why? Because God is always at work behind the scenes, making sure that, in the end, everything will turn out for our good! It's like knowing the ending of a story in advance, and the ending is always a victory for those who love Him. This is such a comforting promise from God! It tells us that, for those who love Him, everything in life—whether it feels like a blessing or a challenge—is being worked out into something that fits perfectly into His bigger plan for us.

Our lives aren't random, and nothing we go through is pointless. Every high and low, every joy and struggle, is part of God's incredible plan to shape us, bless us, and lead us toward something greater. We can hold on to this truth with confidence, knowing that our Creator is working all things for our good, even if we don't see it immediately. When we live in light of this promise, it fuels our faith and gives us hope to face whatever comes our way. No matter what happens, God is doing something amazing through it all.

This trust is grounded in the nature of God Himself—love, eternal, omniscient, and omnipresent. He is far more than an abstract "consciousness" or a distant force; He is a personal and relational being, with intellect, love, and will. It's revealed through His interactions with us, especially through Jesus Christ and the Holy Spirit. As the Creator and Sustainer of all life, His divine knowledge transcends time and space, encompassing every aspect of reality. It is this intimate, active involvement in our lives that allows us to trust Him, even when we don't understand the trials we face.

God's omniscience means He knows the past, present, and future with perfect clarity. The Scriptures declare that He is **"the Alpha and the Omega, the First and the Last, the Beginning and the End"** (Revelation 22:13). He sees all things, both great and small, with nothing hidden from His sight. Every event in our lives, every decision we make, unfolds according to His divine purpose. We may not always understand why things happen the way they do, but we can rest assured that God's wisdom surpasses our understanding.

When we think of God's control over all things, it can be too overwhelming for our human minds. We have limited knowledge and often struggle to understand how our Holy Heavenly Father governs the universe and our lives. I have found it difficult at times to fully grasp how He can be in control of everything—literally everything at the same time! Yet, the more we learn about God and His ways, the more our perspective shifts. Instead of looking at life through the lens of fear, we begin to view everything through faith, trusting in the Supreme order that He has established.

God is not only our Creator but also our Sustainer. His involvement in creation is neither distant nor mechanical. He is not an uninterested ruler who watches from the heavens, indifferent to what happens on earth. No, God is intimately involved in every detail of His creation, from the vast galaxies down to the smallest cells in our bodies. Every aspect of creation—from the complex ecosystems to the smallest creatures—has been given order and purpose by God's hand. Nothing is random. Everything He made interacts in perfect harmony because He sustains it with His wisdom and providence.

This divine order and harmony are beautifully illustrated in Psalm 148:7-10 (NIV), where the psalmist paints a picture of how all elements of nature obey God's commands and praise Him: **"Praise the LORD from the earth, you great sea creatures and all ocean depths, lightning and hail, snow and clouds, stormy winds that do his bidding, you mountains and all hills, fruit trees and all cedars, wild animals and all cattle, small creatures and flying birds."**

Everything in creation—from the roaring winds to the towering mountains, from the largest sea creatures to the tiniest birds—submits to God's supreme authority and reflects His glory. Nature, in all its beauty and power, is a testament to God's presence and His control over all things.

And if even the elements of nature obey His command and reflect His glory, how much more should we, His children, created in His image, trust Him with our lives? Think about that for a moment: the mountains do not question their height; the winds do not resist their path; the oceans do not doubt their borders. Everything in nature surrenders to God's will and fulfills its purpose. Shouldn't we do the same, knowing we were created not only with purpose but with eternal value?

To help you soak in this truth more deeply, I encourage you to take a moment and listen to "Holy Forever" by Alli Gailey on the ALL IN CHRIST YouTube channel. Let the lyrics minister to your soul as they echo the holiness of our Creator—the same God Who commands the stars and yet tenderly calls you His own.

In reflecting on Job's story and my lessons, it becomes clear that we are often like the turtles in my vision— seemingly small and insignificant, but part of a much grander plan that we cannot fully comprehend. Just as the turtles instinctively follow their path to the sea, we are called to trust in the Sovereignty and Wisdom of God, even when His ways remain a mystery to us. Job's suffering and the divine revelation I received teach us that, though we may question or struggle with the complexities of life, God's purpose is always at work, orchestrating every detail with perfect wisdom. His eternal knowledge transcends our understanding. Just as nature, in all its beauty and power, submits to God's will, we too, are called to trust Him with our lives, embracing His guidance even in the face of hardship. Ultimately, it is through trusting in His goodness, even when we don't have all the answers, that we find peace, knowing that He is not distant or detached, but actively involved in every detail of our existence.

Chapter 24

A Vision of a Mountain

Another vision I had was of a mountain standing tall beneath a pinkish night sky dotted with stars. At first, I didn't fully understand its significance, but a week later, I came across Matthew 17:20 (NIV): **"Truly I tell you, if you have faith as small as a mustard seed, you can say to this mountain, 'Move from here to there,' and it will move. Nothing will be impossible for you."**

God was teaching me here that it's not the size of your faith that matters, but its presence and sincerity. Even a seemingly insignificant amount of genuine faith can unleash incredible power when placed in God. The "mountain" in my vision represented the challenges, obstacles, and seemingly impossible situations we face in life. But through faith, what seems insurmountable can be overcome because God's power is limitless.

About a month after this vision, I found myself suddenly facing a divorce, and a series of other extremely difficult situations unfolded. Despite the overwhelming challenges, I could feel God's presence surrounding me, enveloping me with His love and comfort. His support was all around me, and though I was walking through one of the hardest times of my life, the peace I felt in my heart was indescribable! It was a peace that defied all understanding, a calmness that I could only attribute to His unwavering presence. I could literally feel His comforting embrace, strengthening me every step of the way. The more I leaned into Him, the more I realized that no matter how stormy the circumstances, His peace was a constant, and His love never wavered.

When you are in Christ, He becomes your sustainer, protector, and provider. His blessed love and faithfulness never waver for those who place their trust in Him. Cling to Him with all your heart, for He will never fail you. Even in the darkest moments, when life feels overwhelming, His strength remains constant, and His promises are sure. All He asks is for a little faith—a faith as small as a mustard seed. Even this small measure of faith can move mountains, transforming even the bleakest circumstances into opportunities for growth and God's power to shine.

Chapter 25

Jesus' Divine Feet

One day, as I was driving and pouring out my heart to Jesus—overwhelmed by my life situation—I felt a deep longing for a response from Him. In a moment of vulnerability, I chuckled at the thought that I sometimes felt like I was merely talking to myself. But the very next morning, God revealed His divine feet to me, adorned in brown leather sandals. I received this vision about a month after seeing a vision of a mountain. This revelation struck me profoundly. I sensed that He was inviting me to walk with Him in faith—a personal reminder that He is always near, listening to every word I utter. It also felt like a gentle call to bring everything to His feet, to lay down every burden and concern I had been carrying.

In Matthew 15:30-31 (NKJV), we see a powerful image of people bringing their burdens to Jesus, laying them down at His feet for healing and restoration: **"Then great multitudes came to Him, having with them the lame, blind, mute, maimed, and many others; and they laid them down at Jesus' feet, and He healed them. So the multitude marveled when they saw the mute speaking, the maimed made whole, the lame walking, and the blind seeing; and they glorified the God of Israel."**

Reading this passage helped me understand what I had seen. Those people brought their brokenness to Jesus and laid it down—literally—at His precious feet. And He met them there with healing and power. I realized that I could do the same. I didn't need to carry my pain alone or have everything figured out. I could simply come as I was.

But that vision was about more than comfort—it was a call. A call to take my first steps in truly trusting Him. I felt Jesus inviting me to begin the journey of walking with Him, even if I didn't know where the path would lead. He wasn't asking for perfection—just surrender, just a step.

I didn't just see His feet—I sensed Him saying, "Come." Come forward. Come closer. Come freely. Not once did He push or demand; it was a gentle, holy invitation to walk with Him and let Him lead. Jesus is a gentleman—He will never force Himself on you. He waits patiently, offering love without pressure and truth without manipulation. His presence is inviting, not imposing. He honors your **free will** because what He desires most is a **willing heart**. A heart that chooses Him **not** out of fear or obligation, but because it has seen His kindness—and can't help but respond.

Chapter 26

Empty Tomb

On April 1, 2024, that same year, I experienced another incredibly vivid and miraculous vision—a vision of an empty tomb, an undeniable testament to Christ's resurrection! At first, I couldn't fully grasp what I was seeing. It was like I was looking at a large round rock that resembled a door. Then suddenly, I found myself inside, looking at the hay, where a subtle impression remained, as if someone had just been there—yet now, the space was empty. Completely empty.

Just a week later, I came across that very tomb in the Bible, and it hit me with incredible force: **Jesus Christ truly rose from the dead!** This wasn't just a vision—it was a personal confirmation. The resurrection I had once only heard about wasn't just part of a tradition—it was real. It was alive in me now. Jesus conquered death, and because of that, we are invited into a brand-new life. He is risen, and that's why we are risen with Him! Hallelujah!

What an unbelievably surreal experience it was to witness this empty tomb! Moments like these shatter any lingering doubts about the authenticity of God's Word. The resurrection isn't a symbolic tale or a spiritual metaphor. It's history. It happened. And it still happens every day—in hearts that come alive in Him. The tomb is empty, and our hope is full.

Here is an interesting fact to consider: it wasn't just the disciples who witnessed this miraculous event—**over 500 people** saw Jesus alive after His resurrection. As the apostle

Paul wrote in 1 Corinthians 15:6, **"After that, He appeared to more than five hundred of the brothers and sisters at the same time…"** This wasn't a private event, but something witnessed by many—confirming not only the truth of His resurrection, but also what I saw in my vision.

My beloved, I invite you now to take a moment to listen to "What I See" by Elevation Worship. This song has a way of igniting that same excitement and joy that flows through the hearts of believers when we remember the triumph of Jesus over death and sin. Look it up, and let it resonate in your soul. Together, we can celebrate this miraculous truth and join with other believers, allowing the joy of the resurrection to fill us with blessed hope and courage!

Chapter 27

Vision of a Golden Needle

One evening, as I prayed and sought answers about a particular situation in my life, I received a response the very next day in the form of a vision while I was fully awake as it was in the middle of the day. I saw a beautiful bright golden needle very slowly moving across my face, its eye clearly visible. Behind it was an image that was difficult to describe, but it appeared as a sinister figure with the tongue of a snake. This vision reminded me of a powerful teaching of Jesus in Matthew 19, where He speaks about the difficulty of entering the Kingdom of God for those who are attached to earthly wealth and possessions. Jesus' words highlight the challenge of letting go of what ties us to the world, and the necessity of surrendering all to Him in order to fully embrace His Kingdom.

In Matthew 19:23-24 (NIV), it's written, **"Then Jesus said to His disciples, 'Truly I tell you, it is hard for someone who is rich to enter the Kingdom of Heaven. Again I tell you, it is easier for a camel to go through the eye of a needle than for someone who is rich to enter the Kingdom of God.'"** Jesus was illustrating the challenge of entering God's Kingdom for those who are overly focused on material wealth and the things of this world. The image of a camel passing through the eye of a needle emphasizes the impossibility of achieving salvation through wealth or self-sufficiency alone.

However, this teaching is not meant to discourage or condemn, but to point to the necessity of surrendering all things—wealth, pride, and self-reliance—to God. It's a reminder that entrance into the Kingdom of Heaven is not earned by human effort or possessions, but by God's Grace alone. In the next verses, Matthew 19:25-26, Jesus assures His disciples that with man it is impossible, but with God, all things are possible: **"When the disciples heard this, they were greatly astonished and asked, 'Who then can be saved?' Jesus looked at them and said, 'With man this is impossible, but with God all things are possible.'"**

As mentioned earlier in this book, salvation is a divine work that only God Himself can accomplish. No one can earn it through their strength, wealth, or achievements. It is a gift from God, available to all who humble themselves and rely on His grace. Jesus' teaching calls us to examine our hearts and priorities. Are we clinging to the things of this world, or are we ready to give them up to fully follow Christ? The eye of the needle in my vision could symbolize this very challenge—reminding us that, while the path to God's Kingdom may seem narrow, God's Grace is sufficient to carry us through.

My dear friends, let this powerful teaching from Matthew 19 stir your heart to reflect honestly: What are you holding onto that might be keeping you from fully following Christ? Is it comfort, pride, control, or something else entirely? Remember His words: **"With man this is impossible, but with God all things are possible."** Whatever seems too hard to let go of, He can help you release. Let it go—and let God in.

Chapter 28

Are You Not Much More Valuable Than the Birds?

On December 26th, 2024, the day after Christmas, I found myself alone in my room, weighed down by financial worries that pressed heavily on my heart. With my eyes closed, I prayed earnestly, seeking God's guidance and help, unsure of how I would navigate the uncertain road ahead. The bills were piling up, and doubt clouded my thoughts. Yet, in the midst of it all, a deep sense of peace washed over me, as if God was drawing near. And then, in that stillness, a vision unfolded before me. I saw a bird, calmly pecking at the grains scattered across the earth. It moved with ease, unburdened, without a care in the world. The scene was simple, yet profoundly beautiful. In that moment, I felt a quiet whisper in my heart, reminding me of God's tender care—even for the smallest of His creatures.

As I looked at that bird, the words of Jesus echoed in my mind: **"Look at the birds of the air; they do not sow or reap or store away in barns, and yet your heavenly Father feeds them. Are you not much more valuable than they?"** (Matthew 6:26, NIV). The verse came alive in my heart, and I realized that even in times of financial uncertainty, God is always present, providing for His creation.

My vision and the verse from Matthew 6 are deeply intertwined, offering both comfort and perspective. The bird feeding on the grains is symbolic of God's constant provision. The bird doesn't worry about where its food will come from, and in the same way, I was being reminded that God has already made a way for me, even if I cannot see it clearly right now. This vision is an invitation to all of us to release our anxieties into God's care, trusting that He will provide for us in ways that may surprise us. And sure enough, God showed up in my life and showed off! Again and again, supernaturally, I was provided for over and over. Bills were paid when I couldn't see how they'd be covered and opportunities I hadn't anticipated appeared right when I needed them most. It wasn't just that my needs were met— God went beyond that, providing not only for what I *thought* I needed, but also blessing me with more than I could have imagined. There were moments of grace that I couldn't explain, moments where I knew with certainty that God's hand was at work, orchestrating every detail.

In hindsight, I can see that His provision wasn't just about financial stability; it was about deepening my trust in Him, about learning that His care is far greater than my worries, and that when we release control, He will step in to show us just how much He can do. What began as a moment of anxiety and uncertainty transformed into a powerful testimony of God's faithfulness. Even when the path ahead seemed unclear, God made a way. And in the end, His provision was far more abundant than I could have ever anticipated. His timing was perfect, and His blessings exceeded my expectations, teaching me that when we truly trust Him, we'll see how He can do immeasurably more than we could ask or imagine.

God is not asking for much—just a small, simple trust in Him, and with that, He can do great and mighty things in our lives. The opposite is also true: if we lack faith in God or do not believe that all things are possible through Him alone, it becomes difficult for God to work in our lives. Even Jesus, during His earthly ministry, chose not to perform miracles or could not do many miracles in places where there was no faith. In Matthew 13:58 (NIV), it says, **"And He did not do many miracles there because of their lack of faith."** Similarly, in Mark 6:5-6 (NIV), it states, **"He could not do any miracles there, except lay His hands on a few sick people and heal them. He was amazed at their lack of faith."** These passages show us that our belief plays a crucial role in what God can do for us. When we trust Him, even with the smallest amount of faith, He is able to move mountains in our lives, but without faith, even the power of God seems restrained. Remember: It's impossible to please God without placing our faith in Him only.

This emphasizes the importance of trusting God and having faith that He can do the impossible. When we take that step of trust, no matter how small, we open the door for God to work in mighty ways.

As Matthew 6:31-33 (NIV) continues: **"So do not worry, saying, 'What shall we eat?' or 'What shall we drink?' or 'What shall we wear?' For the pagans run after all these things, and your heavenly Father knows that you need them. But seek *first* His Kingdom and His righteousness, and all these things will be given to you as well."**

I have learned, through both struggle and provision, that seeking God first is not a mere suggestion but a divine principle. It's easy to make the mistake of seeking solutions before seeking His presence, but I've found that when we put

God at the center, all things—our needs, desires, and even our understanding—begin to align with His purpose. Our struggles may not disappear overnight, but the peace and assurance that follow His guidance bring us closer to the abundant life He promises.

Chapter 29

He Stands for You: A God Who Comforts

Just before my divorce was finalized, I had a vision I will never forget: I saw our Heavenly Father rise from His throne and move swiftly toward me. Startled, I opened my eyes in wonder, unsure why such a powerful image came at that exact moment. Later that month, I came across a testimony by Camille Gent, who shared a near-death experience strikingly similar—God the Father standing up from His throne to comfort her in deep heartbreak. He told her He does this every time His beloved children are hurting—we simply don't see it.

Later, it was confirmed by the Word of God that one of the many reasons why God could stand from His throne is mentioned in Psalm 102:13 (NIV): **"You will arise and have compassion on Zion, for it is time to show favor to her; the appointed time has come."**

In this verse, *Zion* refers to more than just a physical location—it represents **God's people**, His covenant family, those who belong to Him. In biblical terms, Zion often symbolizes Jerusalem, the heart of worship and God's dwelling place, but spiritually, it points to *His beloved children*—those who seek Him, trust Him, and are called by His name. So when the Psalm says that God will "arise and have compassion on Zion," it is a powerful picture of the LORD **rising in mercy and love to comfort, defend, and show**

favor to His hurting people—just like He is doing for me in that moment of deep pain.

Not long after that vision, and only a month after my divorce was finalized—before I could even begin to heal—I received devastating news: my mom had been diagnosed with the final stage of a very aggressive pancreatic cancer. My heart shattered all over again. The grief hit me like a wave, and for a moment, I felt frozen—panic, disbelief, and exhaustion all swirling inside me. I kept asking, Why? How could this be? But slowly, as I clung to God's promises, those raw emotions softened. I began to feel a fragile hope rising beneath the pain, anchored by the vision of God moving toward me.

Even now—as I write these words in a dark and uncertain season—the LORD, the God of peace, is covering me with a supernatural calm only He can give. It's the very peace described in Philippians 4:6–7 (NKJV): **"Be anxious for nothing, but in everything by prayer and supplication, with thanksgiving, let your requests be made known to God; and the peace of God, which surpasses all understanding, will guard your hearts and minds through Christ Jesus."**

I had read that passage many times, but only living it revealed its power. This peace isn't just the absence of anxiety—it's a steady, unshakable presence. Like a deep ocean beneath stormy skies, calm and constant, it holds me even when fear crashes around me. One night, overwhelmed by worry, I prayed and felt that quiet peace settle over me like a warm blanket. It didn't erase the storm, but it gave me strength to face it.

What's even more incredible? That same peace is now touching my mom's life too! After lifting her up in prayer repeatedly—pleading for mercy—she called me a few days ago and said something that made my jaw drop. She told me she had experienced God's presence like never before in her life. For the first time ever! Hallelujah! God heard my prayers! He's reaching out, moving in her heart in ways only He can. She described it as a wave of total peace and bliss—like floating on a cloud wrapped in comfort and worship. (Okay, maybe not those exact words, but that's what it felt like to her—and to me, it was the most beautiful thing.) That conversation renewed my hope and gave me fresh strength for the tough days ahead. See, this proves that when we press in, praying and pleading for those we love, God listens. He honors our prayers. Even when it takes time—even when it feels like we're talking to the ceiling—He is always working behind the scenes, touching hearts in ways we could never imagine.

Beyond this supernatural peace that surpasses understanding, knowing the truth has brought countless blessings into my life. One of the greatest is this: I now know—without a shadow of a doubt—that heaven is real. That alone has given me a deeper layer of comfort than I ever thought possible. I honestly can't imagine walking through this season without the assurance that God is real, His promises true, and that eternal life awaits those who belong to Him. It changed my daily life in practical ways— reminding me to cherish moments, forgive more quickly, and love more deeply.

When God opens your eyes to the truth, everything changes—even the way you see death. What once seemed terrifying and final now becomes a doorway into everlasting life. The Holy Spirit keeps reminding me that death is not the end for those who belong to Jesus—it's the beginning of something far greater. That truth has loosened the grip of fear from my heart and wrapped my grief in hope. What used to bring sorrow now brings peace, because I now know that God has already written the final chapter—and it ends in eternal life, not goodbye.

I feel truly blessed that God revealed Himself and His salvation to me two years ago—just before everything in my life began to fall apart. That timing wasn't random; it was **Grace**. Because of that revelation, I now carry God's perfect peace that I couldn't have found on my own. Whether God chooses to heal my mom completely here on earth or welcome her into eternal rest, I have assurance in Him. And by His mercy, my mom shares in that same peace too—not a momentary comfort, but a deep, enduring calm that anchors the soul.

And honestly? Now, trusting God feels natural—effortless even—because I know **my mom is in the best hands possible**. He continues to whisper truth to my heart with the gentleness of a loving Father comforting His child. And the more I've seen of Him, the more I've learned to let go. I've surrendered this entire situation into His hands, knowing that the One Who has already blessed me beyond measure will never fail me. So I can say with confidence and quiet strength: I trust Him—fully, completely, and without fear. Because He's always been faithful. And He always will be.

I remember one morning when fear tried to consume me, and all I could pray was, "LORD, I can't handle this anymore! I give it all to You." That raw, desperate moment became a turning point. Choosing faith over fear wasn't easy, but it was necessary. Since then, surrender has looked like trusting Him with both the little things and the life-changing ones—even when I can't see what's ahead. It's a daily choice to rest in His control instead of reaching for my own. And every time I do, His peace meets me there—faithful, steady, and strong.

If Jesus has carried me through my darkest valleys—bringing peace and comfort that truly surpass all understanding—then He can do the same for you... and even more.

Remember these words from Isaiah 41:10 (NKJV), spoken just for you today:

"Fear not, for I AM with you;
Be not dismayed, for I AM your God.
I will strengthen you,
Yes, I will help you,
I will uphold you with My righteous right hand."

These aren't just words on a page—they are promises meant to come alive in your life. When grief overwhelms you, He will be your strength. When uncertainty clouds your mind, He will uphold you. When peace feels impossible, He offers you His perfect peace. This is Who our God is: faithful, ever-present, and unshakably good—even in your darkest hour.

Because of this truth, you can stand—not in your own strength, but upheld by His righteous right hand. And that will always be enough. Without Him, we would fall—but with Him, we are unshakable.

Chapter 30

Hearing God: My Sheep Hear My Voice

In the quiet moments of my journey, I began to experience more of these truly extraordinary audible insights from our LORD Jesus Christ Himself. These were not mere thoughts or random voices, but clear, distinct words directly spoken to me or, sometimes, through my daughter, often quoting Scripture. I came to understand that this is one of the ways Jesus communicates with His followers—through His Word, bringing it to life in a deeply personal and audible way. As Jesus declares in John 10:27 (NKJV), **"My sheep hear My voice, and I know them, and they follow Me,"** I understood deeply that I am His, and He has made His voice known to me.

It was a profound confirmation of my relationship with Him, just as John 5:25 (NIV) affirms, **"Very truly I tell you, a time is coming and has now come when the dead will hear the voice of the Son of God, and those who hear will live."** Through these divine encounters, I was awakened to a new depth of intimacy with Christ, as He called me closer, guiding me with His living Word. What I am about to share is not just a personal reflection, but a testament to the powerful, life-giving voice of God, speaking through His Word to guide and transform His adopted children. While some of the audible insights were deeply personal, I am sharing here those that are most relevant and meaningful for you—lessons that you, too, can learn from and apply in your own life.

God has shown me that these revelations are not for me to keep to myself, but rather, they are meant to awaken hearts and minds to the truth—the only truth that matters. He desires for us to boldly proclaim that God is real, Jesus is alive, and heaven is waiting for those who choose to believe. Just as Matthew 10:27 says, **"What I tell you in the dark, speak in the daylight; what is whispered in your ear, proclaim from the rooftops,"** these messages are not just for my benefit—they are entrusted to me to share openly with others. God compels me to proclaim the good news, to help others see the depth of His love, and to reveal the truth of His Kingdom.

Chapter 31

"You Are Worthy"

There was a time when I struggled deeply with feelings of unworthiness. I wrestled in my mind, questioning how someone like me, with all my flaws and failures, could be worthy of Jesus' love and salvation. I felt unworthy of His grace, unworthy of His sacrifice, and unsure if I even deserved to be saved. In the midst of that quiet storm of doubt, something incredible happened. Out of nowhere, my two-year-old daughter, Sophia, who was far too young to understand the weight of such words, suddenly uttered, "You are worthy." I was speechless.

How could she know what I was thinking at that **exact perfect moment**? I hadn't said a word—no one had heard the doubts swirling in my mind. How could she, at such a young age, know to say something like that?! I had never spoken those words to her before, nor was it something I would typically say. It seemed impossible that she could have understood the depth of my internal struggle, yet there she was, speaking the very words I so desperately needed to hear at that very moment! I suddenly knew it was a divine message from Jesus Himself. It was as though He was gently reminding me that my worth is not defined by my perceived shortcomings, doubts, or the world's opinions of me. It was rooted in His love and the willing sacrifice He made for me on the cross.

The truth is, none of us are inherently worthy of salvation. But when we choose Jesus, we are made worthy through

Him. In the New Testament, worthiness is not based on personal perfection, but on faith, righteousness, and a life dedicated to Christ. It is Jesus' sacrifice and God's calling that make us acceptable before Him. As 2 Corinthians 5:21 (NKJV) declares, **"For He made Him Who knew no sin to be sin for us, that we might become the righteousness of God in Him."** Jesus, though sinless, took our sin upon Himself so that we could be made righteous—made worthy—through Him. Our worthiness does not come from anything we've done, but from everything He's done for us.

This reality became even clearer to me through my personal experience with God. I had been battling feelings of unworthiness, but through the Scriptures and the Holy Spirit, I came to understand that when we accept Jesus into our lives, we are made victorious. Our worth is no longer determined by our flaws, past or future mistakes, or by the fleeting standards of the world. Instead, it is defined by the unwavering love of Jesus and His grace, which covers all who are saved. We no longer need to question our value, for we have been adopted into God's perfect family as His beloved children, secure in His love and eternal care.

The key takeaway from this divine revelation is this: **Jesus is the One Who makes us worthy.** When we place our trust in Him, we are no longer defined by our imperfections or the labels of this world. As Romans 8:31 proclaims, **"If God is for us, who can be against us?"** What a tremendous privilege it is to be on God's team—not the world's—for our identity and worth are secure in Him, no matter how people around us may see us. The world may try to tell you who you are, but only Jesus gets the final word—and in Him, that word is *worthy*.

This truth comes alive beautifully in the worship song "Who Else," performed by Alli Gailey (originally by Gateway Worship). You can find it on YouTube. These lyrics will speak directly to your heart. They reflect the sovereignty of God and the irreplaceable reality that there is no one else who can compare to Him. It's more than a song—it's an invitation to worship God wholeheartedly, acknowledging that **only** He is worthy of our praise. Let the music carry you into His presence, where the truth of our identity and worth in Christ is reaffirmed in the most beautiful way.

Chapter 32

"The Work in Your Heart Will Be Brought to Completion"

One day, I found myself beating myself up over making the same sinful mistakes yet again. I was overwhelmed with shame, guilt, and self-doubt when, out of nowhere, I heard a tender voice say, "The work in your heart will be brought to completion." It took me completely by surprise, and in that moment, an overwhelming wave of relief washed over me. Jesus Himself was comforting me, gently reminding me that despite my flaws, He was still at work within me. This process—what the Bible calls **sanctification or purification**—is the lifelong journey of being made new from the inside out. It's not about perfection, but about progress through His grace.

The very next thing I did was open the Word of God—eager to understand the message I had just received—and sure enough, there it was, clear as day. Philippians 1:6 (ESV) says, **"And I am sure of this, that He Who began a good work in you will bring it to completion at the day of Jesus Christ."** Those words wrapped around my heart like a warm blanket. God wasn't done with me—not even close. In fact, it felt like He was rolling up His sleeves and saying, "Just getting started!" Or, as I like to think of it—He was just warming up.

Later, I discovered 1 Thessalonians 5:23-24 (NKJV), which affirmed the same truth: **"Now may the God of** peace Himself sanctify you completely; and may your whole spirit, soul, and body be preserved blameless at the coming of our LORD Jesus Christ. He Who calls you is faithful, Who also will do it." Now I knew, without a doubt, that God's work in me is far from finished and will continue to be perfected until the return of Christ Jesus.

God was teaching me that He will perfect and complete the work He has started, not just in me, but in every believer filled with His Holy Spirit. What a comfort to know that, despite our stumbles along the way, our Holy Father continues to shape us and build our character into something strong and steadfast. The key here is to give an honest evaluation of ourselves—acknowledging our weaknesses and being ready to admit them before God. It is in this humility that we become **most useful to Him.**

He's not looking for perfection—He's looking for a willing heart. He desires partnership with those who are honest with Him, surrendered, and **teachable**. This sanctification doesn't happen all at once; it's a lifelong journey of becoming more like Christ. Step by step, as we walk with Him, He shapes our hearts, strengthens our character, and leads us toward spiritual maturity—until we are fully conformed to the image of Christ.

As 2 Corinthians 3:18 (AMP) enlightens us, **"And we all, with unveiled face, continually seeing as in a mirror the glory of the LORD, are progressively being transformed into His image from one degree of glory to even more glory, which comes from the LORD, Who is the Spirit."** This verse beautifully connects to the process of transformation described earlier in this book—God is continually molding us into the likeness of Christ. Through

His Spirit, we are being changed from glory to glory, step by step, until we reach full maturity in Him.

So if you ever catch yourself thinking, "I should be further along by now," take a deep breath and remember: God's not panicking—so why should you? Sanctification isn't a race; it's a walk... and sometimes a crawl... and other times, let's be honest, it's just lying flat on the floor whispering, "Help me, Jesus." But even then, He's still at work. He hasn't given up on you—and He never will. The same God Who began the good work in you isn't done. Not today. Not tomorrow. He's still shaping your heart, and still saying, "My child, I'm not finished with you yet. I'm just getting started." And what a glorious ending He has in store for us!

Chapter 33

"For My Yoke is Easy and My Burden is Light"

In September of 2024, weighed down by the pressures and worries of life, I clearly heard a powerful message from Jesus, like a gentle whisper in my ear: "For My yoke is easy, and My burden is light." I instantly recognized His voice—these were His very words, straight from Scripture. This beautiful promise is found in Matthew 11:28–30 (NIV): **"Come to Me, all you who are weary and burdened, and I will give you rest. Take My yoke upon you and learn from Me, for I AM gentle and humble in heart, and you will find rest for your souls. For My yoke is easy and My burden is light."**

What's absolutely amazing is that, not long after, another believer—someone also walking closely with Christ—told me, before I even said a word, that they had received the exact same verse around the exact same time. Coincidence? Not a chance. God was confirming His Word and letting me know: yes, this was Him speaking. Yes, I was hearing right. Yes, I was not alone. And honestly, just knowing that made me want to laugh and cry at the same time. God is so personal and precise. He knows just how to show up and show off.

Here was Jesus, broadcasting the same invitation to His children all at once: "Come to Me. Rest." Not just rest like a Sunday nap (though those are holy too!), but soul rest. The kind that doesn't fade when the alarm clock goes off the next morning.

And that's exactly what I did.

I came to Him with my weary heart, and sure enough, He did exactly what He promised. Once I made the decision to come to Him in prayer and lay down my burdens (as messy and tangled as they were), something supernatural began to happen. Within the next month or so, I began to see God's hand move in ways I never expected. One of the most miraculous moments involved a burden I had carried for years—the kind that quietly weighs on you day after day. You know the kind... one of those "Why can't this just disappear already?" struggles.

Now, I wish I could share all the details with you, but some things are just too personal to put on paper. What I *can* say is this: as I pressed into prayer and laid it before God, something shifted. Out of what felt like nowhere, a door opened. A way forward appeared. And I knew it wasn't coincidence, luck, or clever maneuvering on my part. It was all Him.

That impossible weight I had been dragging around? Lifted. Handled. And not in the way I had imagined, but in a way that left me standing there like, "Wait... did that just happen?" It did. And it was all God.

So I testify to you now—God is faithful. He means what He says. When He invites us to lay our burdens down, He's not just being poetic. He's being real. He doesn't play games or offer empty promises. He will meet you right in the middle of your mess, lift what's too heavy to carry, and replace it with His supernatural peace.

His yoke really is easy.
His burden really is light.

It doesn't mean life suddenly becomes a breezy walk through a flower field with harp music playing in the background. (If only!) But it does mean you're no longer carrying the load alone. You're yoked to Jesus—the One Who already bore the heaviest burden of all on the cross. And with Him, nothing is impossible.

So, if you're tired, burnt out, or carrying something that feels way too big to manage, take Him at His word. Come to Him. Drop the backpack of fear, shame, pride, control, or whatever else you've been hauling around. Let Him carry it. Let Him carry *you*.

And who knows? You might just hear that same whisper in your ear:
"For My yoke is easy, and My burden is light."

And when it happens, you'll smile—not because the path got easier, but because the weight is no longer yours. It's His.

Chapter 34

"Rejoice Always"

One morning, while driving and feeling especially down and irritable, I received a clear and powerful word from the LORD: "Rejoice always." It stopped me in my tracks. It was as if He was gently realigning my heart in the middle of my frustration. I realized in that moment that joy is not just a feeling; it's a decision to align our hearts with God's will, regardless of how we feel or what we're facing. The LORD was teaching me that joy is not based on external circumstances but rooted in Him.

This truth echoed what Scripture declares in 1 Thessalonians 5:16–18 (NIV): **"Rejoice always, pray continually, give thanks in all circumstances; for this is God's will for you in Christ Jesus."** God's will is not for us to live in defeat or discouragement, but to rejoice—even when things don't go our way—because we belong to Him. And not only do we belong to Him, but we are also awaiting the most glorious event in all of human history: **the return of our King of Glory, Jesus Christ.**

As believers, we are not living for this world alone. We are looking ahead with joyful anticipation because our Redeemer is coming back for us. This is not wishful thinking—it is a blessed promise sealed in God's Word. Titus 2:13 (NIV) encourages us to **"wait for the blessed hope—the appearing of the glory of our Great God and Savior, Jesus Christ."** That hope is what strengthens us in our trials and causes joy to rise even in suffering.

We can rejoice always because the King above all kings and the LORD above all lords is coming soon—this time, not to suffer, but to reign in glory. Jesus Himself said in Revelation 22:12 (NIV): **"Look, I AM coming soon! My reward is with Me, and I will give to each person according to what they have done."** His return will usher in the end of sorrow, pain, and evil. For those who are in Christ, this is not a moment to fear—it is the ultimate fulfillment of every longing heart.

Philippians 4:4 says it plainly: **"Rejoice in the LORD always. I will say it again: Rejoice!"** Why? Because our joy is not anchored in this broken world. It is anchored in the unshakable reality that we will see our Savior face to face. He will wipe every tear from our eyes (Revelation 21:4), and we will dwell in the house of the LORD forever.

Even now, while the world grows darker and more chaotic, our joy shines all the brighter. Jesus told us in John 14:3 (NIV): **"And if I go and prepare a place for you, I will come back and take you to be with Me that you also may be where I AM."** That's a promise from the mouth of our Savior. He is coming back—and that changes everything.

So let this be our anthem: we will rejoice—not because our lives are perfect, but because our hope is certain. Our joy is anchored in the One Who conquered death, rose again, and is returning in glory. No trial, no storm, no failure can take that from us. As children of God, we are not waiting in fear—we are waiting in expectation. Our King is coming. So, brothers and sisters, let our hearts rejoice!

The list of these supernatural visions, audible messages, and miraculous divine wonders goes on and on. If I were to detail every miracle and the intricate experiences of divine encounters since my salvation, I could easily fill many more books with them!

After witnessing these countless miracles and revelations, my faith stands unshakable. There is no force, no voice, and no doubt that can sway me from this truth—God is undeniably real. Jesus willingly sacrificed Himself for our sins on that cross, and the gift of the Holy Spirit pulses with life and power within me. It is more than just a belief; it's a life-changing reality that ignites my very soul! We are called to awaken others to the reality of God's Kingdom, for the truth is here, and it is meant for everyone.

Peace be with you—God's peace. Blessings to you all!

Chapter 35

In Awe of God

I am in awe. There is no other way to describe it.

God, our Almighty Creator, revealed Himself to me—through visions, audible insights, and in ways I can't even put into words. And then, He confirmed His presence through my innocent little girl and through the words of fellow believers. Again and again, the Holy Spirit spoke, reminding me I wasn't imagining any of it. What I encountered was real—undeniably, supernaturally real.

To think that the Creator of the universe would choose to reveal Himself in such a deeply personal way is overwhelming. That He would fill us with His Spirit and make His home within us—what an unimaginable gift! It's so extraordinary that, at times, I struggle to even accept it, not because it's hard to believe, but because it's just that incredible. Every word I try to use to describe this experience feels like a massive understatement.

It's phenomenal. It's surreal. It's absolutely groundbreaking!

This experience isn't just something to understand—it's something that reaches the deepest parts of my soul. My heart overflows with gratitude and reverence. My eyes fill with tears of joy. It's a reality so profound, so overwhelming that it leaves me utterly speechless, yet bursting with excitement! How can anyone truly understand this? How could words possibly do justice? It's the most amazing thing that can ever happen to anyone—to be touched by the living God, to hear His voice, to know that He is real, present, and deeply personal. It's the most life-changing, soul-transforming thing anyone can ever experience. Nothing compares.

Oh, how I long for everyone to experience this indescribable bliss and love—the presence of the living God. If Jesus could reach someone like me, in all my brokenness and doubt, then I know without a shadow of a doubt that He can reach you too. This kind of encounter isn't reserved for the perfect or the privileged. It's for anyone willing to call on His name with a sincere and open heart.

Because just one moment in His presence changes your life entirely. It brings the kind of healing that years of striving, therapy, or self-help could never accomplish. And when it happens, you'll know—your soul has finally come home. You won't be able to stop talking about God, loving Him, worshiping Him. Why? Because **your soul was made to worship Him!**

Be encouraged, my beloved: All you need is God at the center of your life. Everything else will fall into place in His perfect timing. You have nothing to lose—but everything to gain. If you seek fulfillment elsewhere, you will not be satisfied. The highest calling, the greatest success, the most noble achievement in this life is to be reconciled with your Heavenly Father and to receive His Holy Spirit.

There is **no** greater human achievement on earth than this. This is the greatest purpose we can ever fulfill in this life.

And it is all because of Jesus Christ.

Stand in awe of the God Who still reveals Himself, Who

still speaks, Who still saves. To Him alone belong all the praise, all the honor, and all the glory—now and forevermore! Amen.

Now, I invite you to join me to say this final prayer:

Our Heavenly Father, King of Glory, Holy, and Righteous, we humbly come before You. Forgive us for the times we have strayed from Your path, ignored Your voice, and let worldly distractions pull us away from You.

We live in a broken world filled with sin and confusion. Our hearts long to honor You, yet we struggle against doubt, apathy, and indifference. Even when You reveal Your glory, we are often too burdened to fully respond. Save us from ourselves, O LORD!

In a world where truth is distorted and right and wrong are blurred, we ask for Your divine discernment. Open our eyes, ears, and hearts to recognize Your truth. Shine Your light into the darkness so we are no longer deceived.

Awaken hearts everywhere, LORD. Lead the lost back to You. Grant us the precious gift of repentance. We depend on Your mercy and grace, not because we deserve it, but because of Your boundless love and kindness.

O LORD, may You guide us all into deeper communion with You, revealing more of Yourself as we seek Your presence. May the revelation of Your truth take root and bear fruit, transforming lives from the inside out.

O Jesus, please have mercy on us and adopt us into Your perfect Family.

And as we pray for each person reading this, we ask that You grant them the precious gift of Your Holy Spirit—Who leads into all truth. May this seed flourish in their hearts and reflect the love and light of Christ to a world in desperate need.

Thank You, our Holy Heavenly Father, our King of Glory, for hearing our prayers.

In the Mighty Name of Jesus Christ of Nazareth— our LORD and Savior—we pray this. Amen.

About the Author

I'm just an ordinary person who has dedicated most of my adult life to healthcare, grounded in a scientific and mathematical mindset. For most of my life, miracles and supernatural phenomena were things I dismissed as fiction, reserved only for sci-fi movies. The concept of God felt distant and unfamiliar. Yet deep down, I've always felt a yearning for something greater, something beyond the mundane routines of everyday life. I've often hoped that there's more to life than just the ordinary.

I had no real understanding of what salvation meant, nor had I ever pursued it. My upbringing lacked any religious influence—my parents only went to church when times were very tough—and even then, it was rare, maybe once a year. Prayer and church attendance were not part of our home. The concept of salvation was entirely unfamiliar to me—I didn't seek it; I didn't expect it. Yet, somehow, I found it. Remarkably, I was saved without even realizing what was happening—it felt accidental at the time.

It wasn't until after this moment of salvation that I began to understand what had truly happened. Through conversations with other believers—and later, through the Bible itself—I started to grasp the depth of what I had experienced. God confirmed it all through supernatural visions, audible messages, and miracles in which Jesus Christ graciously revealed Himself to me. These experiences affirmed that I wasn't imagining things—they were real, personal, and transformative.

This unexpected, seemingly accidental salvation became the most profound revelation of my life. It confirmed the existence of God, the reality of Jesus Christ, and the undeniable truth that His Word is alive and still speaking—revealing mysteries, imparting wisdom, and proving that God's promises are just as real today as they were then.

As I reflect on my journey, I see how deeply these encounters have reshaped my understanding of life, truth, and reality. What began as a bewildering and unexpected experience has now become the foundation of a life filled with purpose, peace, and unshakable faith. I am no longer the skeptic I once was. Today, I embrace the miraculous—not as fantasy, but as a testament to God's relentless love, grace, and power. It's the greatest privilege to become a witness to such divine truth—one that changed everything, for good and forever.

Now, with a heart full of gratitude and a renewed sense of purpose, I am passionate about sharing my testimony. Whether through writing, speaking, or one-on-one conversations, I hope to inspire others to seek, to question, and to discover their own encounters with the living God. As I continue this journey, I'm committed to walking alongside others—offering the same encouragement and hope I received. No matter where you are in your story, remember: God's love is real, and His salvation is always within reach.

Writing this book has been one of the greatest honors of my life. As you come to the end of these pages, I want to thank you from the bottom of my heart for taking the time to read. It fills me with indescribable joy and deep gratitude to share my personal testimony with you—because more than anything, it's an invitation to experience the love and presence of the living God for yourself. My story is just one reflection of His glory, and I pray it sparks something deep within you to seek Him earnestly.

God bless you all, my beloved, and may His Peace and Grace be with you always! Amen and Amen.

www.ingramcontent.com/pod-product-compliance
Lightning Source LLC
Chambersburg PA
CBHW060054150626
46556CB00017BA/624